ENDO

Perfection! This is the book your clients are hoping you read next! The authors of this book have delivered the pinnacle guide for transforming your career into the practice that will grow in value for you and the clients you love to serve. The style is easy to read, with practical examples of every step necessary to convert and scale your practice into a fee-based enterprise. The sequencing of the book is a master class that provides a road map to transform your service model, fee structure, value proposition, and vision. This is the future state of the greatest advisory practices in our noble profession.

—Kelly Kidwell
CEO, Pacific Advisors LLC

I highly recommend the newly published book *Practice on Purpose*, second edition. It's a must-read for all financial services advisors. It's applicable to people beginning their careers and anyone who has been in practice and can feel in their gut that the world is changing.

It's always helpful to follow those pioneers who got out in front of substantial change at a time when most could not see the future—North Star's management, starting with Phil Richards back in the early '70s; then Ed Deutschlander, the current CEO; and Gary Schwartz, who was instrumental in helping create the curriculum for this transformation.

This book explains—not just theoretically, but step by step—how to transform your practice into a value-added, sustainable program that will allow you to do good, do well by doing good, and be happy doing well by doing good. No wonder The American College has chosen *Practice on Purpose* to be a textbook in the new CLU® curriculum.

—Joseph W. Jordan
Financial Services Speaker, Best-Selling Author

This thoughtfully presented work, *Practice on Purpose* (second edition), is instructional, motivating, actionable, and has cracked the code on successful practice management for financial services practitioners.

When the first edition was released, I provided a copy to my team of financial advisors and managers, as it provided career-changing wisdom to everyone, no matter how new or seasoned.

Recently, when I was tapped to create a course on Financial Planning Practice Management for California Lutheran University's graduate program for Financial Planning MBA and MSFP students, I went straight to *Practice on Purpose*. It was the obvious best choice for our Week #1 curriculum, framing up the entire course to be based on purpose, values, service, and a solid foundation of excellence in practice-management skills and know-how that are forward-facing and career-lasting.

The three authors, Gary, Phil, and Ed, continue to occupy a unique space in our profession, and we are so very fortunate that they have shared with us their expertise, experience, success, and heart. They were trailblazers with the first edition and continue to contribute to our practice-management toolkits with the second edition. Thank you, gentlemen, for your continued gifts to our profession.

—Daralee Barbera, EdD, CFP®, CLF®, ChFC®, CMFC™, CPMBC
President, Diversified Professional Coaching LLC
Financial Planning Program Director, California Lutheran University
Adjunct Professor, The American College
Author, Speaker, Past President of GAMA International

Phil, Ed, and Gary, in *Practice on Purpose*, truly capture the essence of what it takes to enjoy a long, successful career as a financial advisor—never losing sight of your purpose, staying true to your "why," and always remembering what got you out of bed in the morning. They make it clear that what motivated you to begin this rewarding profession is what will keep you there. Among other great insights, they also explain why it's so important to lead with advice, not solutions, and how when done right, the former will naturally lead to the latter. This book is an informative and valuable read for all current and future financial advisors across our entire industry.

—Caroline Feeney
CEO, US Insurance & Retirement Businesses, Prudential Financial

Practice on Purpose awakened my profession to be more purposeful and productive.

With the turn of every page, it was there that a coach was hand in hand with me. Causing me to reflect in my thinking about my daily life career. I was inspired. We are serving our clients in their path to freedom of wealth and health. I experienced firsthand the mission and passion of our teachers, our authors. Thank you for your love to our financial advisors in making a difference.

—Winky Cheung, MBA, LUTCF
President, GAMA Hong Kong

What Phil, Ed, and Gary have put together in this book is life changing for any financial advisor. Finding your "why" and having strength of purpose will allow you to build the financial advice practice you've dreamed of. They take you from start to finish— how to find clients, what questions to ask, what words to use, practice management—literally everything you need to be successful as a financial advisor.

—Tom Hegna, CLU®, ChFC®, CASL®
Economist, Author, and Retirement Expert
Founder of the "Paychecks and Playchecks"
Retirement Approach

I am fortunate, in my position, to meet and engage with the top leaders in our profession. Among them are Gary Schwartz, Ed Deutschlander, and Phil Richards.

Recently I read a draft of the second edition of their upcoming *Practice on Purpose* book. This edition includes many updates and new material. This will be a game changer for advisors and their leaders who want to find greater purpose in their lives and in their financial advice practices.

At North Star, their mission is: Changing Lives, Forever®. Through this book, and its lessons, this will be achieved for firms, advisors, and most importantly, their clients. Congratulations!

—Bonnie L. Godsman
President, Finseca

Many Americans are still trying to get our heads around how the Covid-19 pandemic, which changed our world, our lives, our perspectives, and how we interact with each other. This book is so timely—not just for advisors, but for all of us—in asking the thought-provoking question, "How do you see yourself...especially now?" A great question to start as we all "enter a new/different phase of life."

The book is a great recipe for success, as advisors play such a critical role for their clients. The goal for the authors, as it is for The American College of Financial Services, is to "benefit society." We realize that having such a bold goal, it must always start with you, your core values, and your beliefs. This book gives you a road map for the journey. Also, like the mission of The College, the book can accompany you along the journey of lifelong learning! Read the book and impact others so they live the lives they choose. Then, rest assured that you are benefiting society because of "who you are"!

—George Nichols III
President and CEO, The American College of Financial Services

I personally worked with Gary Schwartz for more than a decade and came to respect him for his business knowledge and years of financial services executive expertise. He has worked with thousands of advisors and financial professionals to help them build more successful advice-based businesses. In this book, he and his colleagues take their collective wisdom and make it practical, actionable, and compelling. If you are a financial services professional who wants to make a difference for your clients, grow your business, and leave a lasting legacy for those you care about, then this book is a *must*-read. My advice: Read it cover to cover, complete the practical exercises, and then *just* execute. This book should be in every advisor's office.

—Bill Williams
EVP, The Personal Advisors Group, Ameriprise Financial

Practice on Purpose is a great book to read, as having been in the financial services industry for three decades myself, I can relate to many of the principles of client engagement that are shared by the authors. I was very impressed with the knowledge and experience of the authors in this book, and I was compelled to think about my own experience and use the discussion questions listed in the chapters to make my practice better. Knowing your clients, knowing what they want, building a good prospect list, and having a good follow-up process are vital to a robust clientele base, and the book made me think about that. Thank you, Phil, Ed, and Gary for sharing this valuable advice with us.

—Aamir Chalisa
Advisory Council Chairman, GAMA Global

Ordinary people learn from their own experience. Smart people learn from the experience of others. Geniuses learn from the brains of the best.

Practice on Purpose gives us the opportunity to learn from the brains of the very best in the business. All three authors are great servant leaders, as well as compassionate teachers.

In this book, Gary Schwartz, Ed Deutschlander, and Phillip C. Richards use their experience from decades of developing and growing North Star Financial Group financial advisors to be one of the very best organizations in the world in teaching new and existing financial advisors. They aspire to attain higher sustainable success; to think, plan, and have a road map; and to execute to attain a successful practice and a fulfilling life. This is accomplished by helping their clients achieve the lives they deserve.

I would like to thank Phil Richards again for kindly helping found GAMA Thailand in 2004, and I would like to thank Gary, Ed, and Phil for authoring this wonderful book; it is one of the best gifts to the financial services business. Many financial advisors and millions of their clients' lives will change forever because of it.

—Montri Saeng-Uraiporn, MBA, LUTCF®, RFC®, CFP®
Coach and Founder, Proactive Training and Consultant Co., Ltd.

PRACTICE ON PURPOSE

ACHIEVE THE FINANCIAL ADVICE PRACTICE YOU DESIRE AND YOUR CLIENTS DESERVE

SECOND EDITION

GARY H. SCHWARTZ, CLU®, ChFC®, CRPC®
WITH PHILLIP C. RICHARDS, CLU®, RHU®, AND
EDWARD G. DEUTSCHLANDER, CLU®, CLF®

ISBN: 978-0-578-28616-7

TABLE OF CONTENTS

FOREWORD

How do you see yourself? This has always been a compelling question for men and women as they move through personal and professional life stages. This book asks this important question of you as a financial professional.

In 1927, Dr. Soloman Huebner founded The American College to dramatically improve the professionalism of insurance and financial advisors. His answer to the question of how one sees oneself was to focus on insurance products and how they interacted with business, law, trusts, wealth management, savings, and retirement… and just as importantly, the process of how an advisor presents herself or himself to clients.

The result was the Chartered Life Underwriter® professional designation, the first ever in the financial services profession. Some 95 years later, more than 110,000 professionals hold the CLU® designation.

As the decades have gone by, more designations have been created. The courses of study include financial planning, special-needs planning, and designations that home in on retirement and wealth planning and management.

Earning professional designations says to clients that continuing education and gaining more technical knowledge is important to you as an advisor—and, in turn, for the benefits to your clients.

The first edition of this book was indeed tremendous, and it achieved international recognition. This second edition is even better, and it promises to guide insurance and financial advisors to meaningful professional success and personal fulfillment.

The Discussion Questions appearing throughout the book provide readers with opportunities to apply the wisdom shared to their own professional practices. I know of no other book that comes close to helping answer the questions, "How do you see yourself?" and "How do your clients see you?" The positive influence this book can have on you and your career is beyond measure.

At The American College of Financial Services, we have included this book as one of the texts in three of our four core CLU® courses. Our students will be answering the Discussion Questions as they apply this material to their practices and to the specific course topics they are studying.

I encourage you to read, then reread this book. Highlight portions, make notes in the margin, answer all the Discussion Questions. Keep it at arm's length for additional study and application. Use it as you mentor new people in the business. Use it to rekindle your passion and your purpose.

Godspeed on your journey.

David F. Pierce, MSFS, MSM, MA, AEP®, CLF®, ChFC®, CLU®
Assistant Professor of Insurance and CLU® Program Director
Charles J. Zimmerman Chair in Life Insurance Education
The American College of Financial Services

WATCHING THE WORLD BECOME NORTH STAR

While North Star has a long history of recruiting, developing, and leading advisors, it really took off in 1969 when Phil Richards bought the firm. Phil, originally from Easton, Pennsylvania, was an executive at Minnesota Mutual Life when he decided to return to the field.

He had a cutting-edge idea to build a firm with content experts in all areas that advisors need to best serve their clients. Hence the North Star Resource Group came to be. He surrounded the advisors with marketing, technology, human resources, professional development, recognition, sales support, disability insurance, life insurance, and investment expertise. The most important job, then, is for the advisor to go out and meet successful people who need financial advice and solutions. In addition to being the founder of North Star Resource Group, Phil is the Executive Chairman of the firm.

In 2016, Edward Deutschlander became CEO after twenty-two years with the firm in recruiting, leadership, and advisor development. Since Ed has taken over as CEO, the firm has continued its rapid growth in new clients, new advisors, and increased support for our advisors—most notably in the areas of financial advice, Medicare, employee benefits, and property and casualty insurance.

I (Gary) have officially been at North Star for the past nine years yet have worked with the firm since the 1970s. Before I joined North Star, I had a significant career at Securian Financial and Ameriprise Financial. I bring forty-five years of experience and wisdom to areas at North Star that drive revenue and advisor growth, as well as strategic planning for the future.

The world is becoming North Star Resource Group. We see more and more organizations, including traditional career firms, banks, wire houses, and notably Registered Investment Advisory firms, moving to this design of advisors being supported by teams of specialists. Think of it as the Mayo Clinic of the financial advising profession. North Star has cracked the code and provides it all under one roof, for both the advisor and the client. Nothing is compromised, as long as someone is part of an advisor/client-centric North Star community rather than attempting to embark on the journey toward financial well-being alone, as a do-it-yourselfer.

If you want to go fast, go it alone, If you want to go far, go together.

For independent advisors to create this level of support on their own, they would need to be running billion-dollar-revenue practices. Yet career changers and recent college graduates who join our firm have this level of support in their first week. More importantly, this is a tent large enough that advisors cannot outgrow the firm, and in turn, their clients cannot outgrow the advisors who are partnered with these resources.

Structurally, we are a hybrid RIA. We also have open-architecture product and services offerings. With our expansive offerings, we can search for the right and best solutions for our clients and advisors. We have built perhaps the most accommodating, robust, and independent model that exists in the marketplace. A race is on for independent and corporate RIAs to build the model we already have.

Advisors and their leaders realize they have a choice: cut price or add value. We are reminded of the old adage, "You can have it fast, you can have it good, you can have it cheap…pick any two." Yet there is another way. We can be in a red ocean of undifferentiated competition, or we can be in a blue ocean where value is created and there is no water bloodied by competition.

The more content specialists we present to our clients, the

greater a resource and value we will be. Where there is superior value, cost is less of a factor, and more importantly, retention of clients will increase because we have multiple products and services in place. And we haven't even mentioned business succession/practice continuation yet, which is another sweet spot because of our teaming with early-career advisors that contributes to asset retention and next-generation growth. (You can read more about this at the end of chapter 7.)

The world is becoming North Star Resource Group. The beautiful thing is, we are already here. The reason is because of the servant leadership culture that has been established and ground into our firm, in which the advisor is our customer. We exist to find, grow, nurture, and serve the advisors of the North Star family. We have no other purpose.

Practice on Purpose: Achieve the Financial Advice Practice You Desire and Your Clients Deserve, second edition, is about creating and building advice-based practices at North Star Resource Group. It has been our pleasure to share this way of thinking and of creating a better client experience for all of us in this profession. It is an idea whose time has come.

INTRODUCTION

Many people will make enough money to have their best life possible. Yet without a compassionate, competent advisor who builds a well-functioning practice offering comprehensive financial advice, they may not realize this life. The financial advisors who have a *clear purpose* in their work are better equipped to provide an exceptional client experience for their clients and contribute to their having the best life possible with the money they have.

Advisors who know their *purpose* will more likely value the advice they give and create a monetary value proposition when they engage with a worthy client. The client, in turn, can then realize the best life possible with the money he or she has.

A Refresher: What Is a "Practice on Purpose"?

In 2014, we published the first edition of this book. In the introduction, we explained the advisors who succeed in this business tend to be *intentional* about building their practices—they build what we call a "Practice on Purpose." That term suggests a double meaning of the word "purpose"—you build your practice around your personal *purpose*, and you build it in an intentional way, on *purpose*. Advisors who live their lives and run their financial services practices on purpose are more likely to experience a relevant and meaningful life journey than those who simply go through the motions, with no real focus, aim, or overarching purpose.

The cover we used on the first edition of this book features an archway leading to an inviting meadow. That artwork is symbolic of the fact that building a Practice on Purpose, based on financial advice, requires a commitment from you, the advisor, and often a mindset shift from the traditional view of an advisor's practice. It requires a *conscious realization* that your advice has the greatest impact on clients beyond anything else you can offer them. That archway, that door, is one that only you, the advisor, can go through once you make that commitment.

Once you go through that door, you will not come back to the way you worked with clients before because your life, your practice, and your clients' enjoyment of you and your advice will be altered for the better. The archway is a metaphor for your realization that your advice has significant value.

It's like anything new we learn in life. When we go through a new thought process, it's like walking through a meadow and making a path for the first time. It feels unusual the first time. It feels new, but as you wear a path in your brain and adopt the new approach, you elevate your practice. You start thinking, "My advice has value. My clients need what I do. They're going to benefit from the knowledge and wisdom I've accumulated through all my client experiences." And before you know it, you have worn a new path in your thinking, and you are going to keep going down that path.

Remember—it's a door only you, the advisor, can go through.

The first edition of our book resonated strongly with advisors throughout North Star Resource Group and beyond. We also created a companion workbook by the same name and focused on the practical strategies in the book to guide advisors in achieving the practices of their dreams.

The book became a textbook at the University of Missouri's College of Financial Planning. For five years, I (Gary) was invited there to share its contents with seniors who were finishing the capstone class of their final year. Our desire to write that book emerged from the fulfillment we derive from coaching advisors whose rewards are a consequence of contributing to the financial well-being of our clients.

Now, having worked with hundreds more advisors since 2014, we have updated many key concepts in that book. We have reinforced some important strategies from it in this update, and we have added valuable new information.

About This Second Edition

The goal of this second edition—which is also for financial advisors and their servant leaders—is to *create and provide superior experiences through personal comprehensive financial advice so your clients—and you—can live their best possible lives. Financial advice can lead you to live your best life possible as well.*

Throughout this book are discussion questions for you to cover with your leader or mentor. We believe taking an active approach to learning these concepts, as opposed to just reading them, will lead you to internalize them and understand them more fully.

This book can change you and your practice, and it can change your clients' lives. Why? Because providing deliberate financial advice has the greatest impact and is the future of this profession.

We are excited to share this information with you. We hope it enables you to improve yourself, your practice, and the lives of your clients, in the spirit of North Star Resource Group's long-time vision—Changing Lives, Forever®.

Never Lose Sight of the Basics

Most businesses—most financial advisors' practices—don't shut down suddenly. They lose sight of the basics, follow some trend, and slowly deteriorate. That's how most businesses, and most relationships as well, fail.

Here is a story that illustrates the importance of staying true to your fundamental purpose.

An accomplished fisherman living in a small fishing village sells his fresh fish at a local market. His small stand has a simple sign over it that says, "Fresh Fish for Sale."

One day, some patrons of the market approach the owner and say, "Do you really need the word 'Fresh' on your sign? We know you wake up early every single morning, you go out and catch fish, you bring back the fresh catch of the day, and you sell it in your market."

He thinks about it and says, "You're right. I don't need the word 'Fresh' on my sign."

He takes the word "Fresh" off the sign. Now it says, "Fish for Sale."

Some time passes, and some other patrons in the market approach the business owner. They say, "Do you really need the words 'for Sale' on your sign? We know you're a for-profit business. We know you sell fish and seafood here. Is that necessary?"

He thinks about it again and says, "Yeah, you're probably right. Let me remove the words 'for Sale' from my sign."

Now he has one word on his sign: "Fish." A few days later, some other patrons approach him. They say, "Do you really need the word 'Fish' on your sign? When we walk by, we can see and smell the fish. We know you sell fish and seafood here. Is that necessary?"

The businessman nods and says, "Yeah, you're probably right."

He takes down his sign that says just "Fish." Now he no longer has a sign above his fish market.

Guess what happened to that business in the next year? It went out of business.

This fisherman, who had a thriving business for years, lost sight of the basics—a little bit at a time—and he failed.

The common denominator of failure is the slow erosion of the fundamentals.

Now, that fisherman didn't remove his entire sign the first time someone asked him about it. If someone had walked up to him and said, "You should take down your sign," he would have said, "You're crazy! I would never do such a thing. Why would I do that?"

But he didn't take the entire sign down right away. He whittled it

4

down, a word or two at a time, until no sign was left.

Once you become clear about what your purpose is as an advisor, stay true to it. Put up guardrails, be vigilant, and protect the integrity of your practice. You will stay and prosper. Stick to the fundamentals: finding, educating, motivating, and inspiring clients. Those are your four fundamental roles as an advisor. They are your gifts to the world.

CHAPTER 1

HOW THIS BOOK WILL CHANGE WHO YOU ARE AND YOUR PRACTICE, IF YOU LET IT

"If your path is difficult, it is because
your purpose is bigger than
you thought."

Unknown

In this book, we are offering our insight into achieving the financial advice practice you desire and your clients deserve.

These are carefully chosen words. It's a two-sided endeavor— when you are clear about your purpose *and* you provide comprehensive financial advice, it benefits you and your clients. It enables you to build the type of practice you desire. It also enables you to create an exceptional experience that changes the trajectory of your clients' lives, both financially and in terms of their overall health, wealth, and happiness.

It's fun to think of how high you can take your practice after you read this book.

Financial Advice Is the Only Area with Increasing Value and Compensation

I have gray hair. I've been doing this for a while. Some aspects of our business have changed greatly over the years.

For example, the compensation rate for our financial products is not increasing. The mutual funds with 12b-1s are gone. Managed money used to produce 2 to 3 percent in IA fees. We're down to 0.8 percent now, and 0.6 percent is the average. Property and casualty premiums and commissions have come down. There are very few life insurance trails (renewals) anymore. Annuity compensation has come down, as has compensation for long-term care and disability insurance. Please understand that reduced costs to the consumer is a good thing; however, compensation for advice and wisdom is necessary as well.

Financial advice is the *only* area in which both the compensation and the value are increasing. As a business owner and professional in the personal financial advice profession, you want to have something in your basket of goods that's actually going up. Financial advice is that category.

Here is our definition of financial advice:

> *Financial advice* is the deliberate outcome of knowing and analyzing your clients' current financial situations; learning their financial goals, hopes, and dreams; and charting a path for them to have the best life possible with the money they have.

The most compelling way the information in this book can benefit you is to recognize that *financial advice is the only type of compensation that's increasing in our profession*. If you do not make financial advice the cornerstone of your practice, you are disadvantaging yourself and are likely to be left behind.

However, our incredible career is not about compensation first. It's about clients and *their* personal and financial success first. When we provide exceptional value, our rewards increase as a result.

Unique Benefits of the Advisor Career

Are you excited about your career? There are significant reasons to be!

The advisor career is unique; it delivers valuable benefits we call "the four I's"—income, independence, impact, and intellectual stimulation. Few other careers offer such an incredible opportunity.

This career also fosters *ikigai*. In Japanese culture, *ikigai* is an ideal state of being. The word combines *iki*, meaning "life," and *gai*, meaning "value" or "worth." The concept of *ikigai* is essentially about finding your purpose in life. It establishes that we can experience a higher sense of well-being when we can do something that meets all four criteria shown in the following diagram: something we love, are good at, the world needs, and we can get paid to do. This activity ideally will be our passion, part of our mission, and the foundation of our vocation or profession. The advisor career fosters *ikigai*.

The Old Way of Doing Business No Longer Works

This book is intended to demonstrate to you the old way of doing business in our profession is becoming obsolete. Financial advice is the best and only way forward.

Even McKinsey & Company, a global management consulting firm that was founded in 1926, attests to the bright future for our profession.

In 2020, McKinsey published a report predicting what wealth

9

management will look like in North America in 2030. The report echoes the theme we have stressed in this book—that a focus on asset management is giving way to a focus on financial advice.

"In the next ten years, advisors will gradually shed their role as investment managers and become more like integrated life/wealth coaches who advise clients on investments, banking, health care, protection, taxes, estate, and financial wellness needs more broadly," the report states. "By 2030, at least 80 percent of advisors will offer goal-based advice, and about half of clients will actively pursue and track bite-sized goals (such as saving for three college credits a month)—and this granular goal tracking will span customers' investment, protection, education, retirement, and broader wellness."[1]

The COVID-19 pandemic disrupted life as we know it in many ways, including those related to finances. Widespread unemployment, uncertainty about the economy, and other factors prompted many people to seek out financial advisors.

Ben Harrison is head of advisor solutions at BNY Mellon's Pershing, which provides global financial solutions to advisors, asset managers, and others in the financial services profession. He says millennials are seeking to collaborate with financial advisors—not just about their finances, but also about critical life decisions. Harrison says that for these investors, "The client–advisor relationship is about collaboration and the experience, not just about investment performance. And they increasingly want that experience to be unique, personal, and digital all at the same time."[2]

More than a century ago, the financial services profession started out with a significant focus on selling insurance. Protecting the financial future of families was the profession's essence and mission. Decades later, insurance lost its appeal for many people going into

---

1. "On the Cusp of Change: North American Wealth Management in 2030," McKinsey & Company, January 22, 2020, https://www.mckinsey.com/industries/financial-services/our-insights/on-the-cusp-of-change-north-american-wealth-management-in-2030.
2. "Op-Ed: There's an Increased Demand for Financial Advice. Are Advisors Up to the Challenge?" Ben Harrison, CNBC, March 22, 20218, https://www.cnbc.com/2021/03/22/can-advisors-meet-the-ever-increasing-demand-for-financial-advice.html.

the career. That's when a new focus on managing assets took hold.

Somewhere along the way, a few visionaries saw the best approach is to focus on *all* aspects of clients' financial situations—not just insurance, and not just assets under management (AUM). That trend toward offering comprehensive financial advice, for some unfathomable reason, has only recently begun to replace those more traditional practice models.

Some call this "holistic advice." *Holistic* refers to entire systems, as opposed to separate parts. Whereas holistic advice never reached critical acceptance with boomers and Generation X, it appears to resonate with Millennials. In 2018, for example, just 9 percent of Millennial investors opted for holistic advice from their advisors. But at the current growth rate, 30 percent of all advisory clients were on track to use it by 2025.[3]

 **Discussion Question**

To what extent do you believe financial advice is the only commodity that is increasing in terms of value to clients and compensation for advisors?

Stop here for a moment, and paraphrase the previous discussion about why financial advice is the pathway to the future in our profession. Practice saying it a few times until you internalize it.

3. "Five Trends Reshaping the Advice Business," Angie Herbers, *ThinkAdvisor*, February 24, 2020, https://www.thinkadvisor.com/2020/02/24/five-trends-changing-the-advice-business/.

The Mind of a Capitalist and the Heart of a Social Worker

Beyond a simple definition, offering financial advice in a way that leads clients to financial wellness requires a unique blend of skills. An effective advisor has *the mind of a capitalist* and *the heart of a social worker*.

Because we live in a capitalist country, numbers are a big part of our business. We do need to know how money works from a mathematical and statistical standpoint. We also have to explain it well so it makes sense to people who are not in our profession. It's important for us to lead clients to understand topics like economics, compound interest, portfolio diversification, risk tolerance, and the accumulation and distribution phases of retirement.

It's almost like a foreign language. If clients don't understand these basic concepts, your advice will be less impactful for them. You have to be able to demystify the complex world of finances so your clients understand what they need to know. This is a first step for them to appreciate your advice.

Yet being a great financial advisor is about much more than knowing the technical aspects of financial planning. A great advisor also needs to have the heart of a social worker. Guiding your clients toward their best financial future requires that you have—and express—compassion, empathy, and concern for them. Top advisors genuinely care about their clients and their clients' families. They want to make their communities better by helping people achieve financial security.

Mitch Anthony is the principal of a training and communication consulting firm that specializes in the financial services and insurance profession. He has written some fantastic books about language and mindset. In one of his newer books, *Life Centered Financial Planning*, he explains why this guidance is actually more important than the numbers: "Today's clients want more from you than being a purveyor of products or an asset allocator. They can get these services elsewhere—and at a much lower cost. By becoming a life-centered financial planner, you can demonstrate your wisdom, experience, and insights and help your client clarify their life transitions, priorities, and goals."[4]

Anthony urges advisors to change their central value proposition to one that is focused on the lives of your clients. He calls that value proposition the "Return on Life™" (ROL). He says the definition of ROL is "to get the best life possible with the money you have."[5]

Financial Advice Leads Clients to Positive Behavior Changes

As an advisor, you are in the habit-formation and behavior-modification business, and both fall into the category of discipline. As you work with your clients, you lead them to form good habits so they can stay the course to financial security. Left to their own devices, most people are their own worst enemy. Unless they have an ongoing advice relationship with an advisor, most clients will not implement financial advice, and they certainly won't do it consistently.

We see many clients who have the resources to achieve financial success, yet they don't make good decisions, or they make decisions at the wrong time, or they base their decisions on emotion, or they don't stay with their game and follow a bigger vision for themselves. Most people have good intentions. They want to do the right thing, but they need a little coaching to follow through with it. This is an area in which you provide tremendous value. You lead your clients to make positive behavior changes and to make wise choices, even when you're not around.

4. Mitch Anthony and Paul Armson, *Life Centered Financial Planning: How to Deliver Value That Will Never Be Undervalued* (Hoboken, New Jersey: John Wiley & Sons Inc., 2020), 18.
5. Ibid.

A Better Way to Be an Advisor: It Starts with Your "Why"

What is your *why*—your purpose—as an advisor? Why do you get up in the morning? Why did you become an advisor? It is important for you to connect with your *why* before you can truly see and appreciate the value you offer your clients.

If you don't think you're a big deal and you don't offer significant value to changing the financial behavior and outcomes of your clients, how can you charge for your advice?

Once you do recognize your value, it will change you and your practice.

One of our top advisors at North Star summed this up in a fantastic way when I went to visit her office one day. She had a beautiful office. I walked in and said, "Why are you an advisor? What's your sense of purpose?"

She said, "There is a better way to be an advisor. Turn around."

I turned around. The wall was covered in corkboard, with hundreds of photos displayed. There were smiling people—her clients—at high school graduations, weddings, christenings for babies, vacations, sporting events—you name it. Her clients had given those photos to her and had given her permission to display them in her office.

She told me, "I look at that wall many times every day. When I have clients sitting with me, I think, 'What picture could I get from them someday?'"

In other words, she couldn't *wait* to talk with her clients and find out what was important to them. Knowing their dreams and goals solidified her sense of purpose.

Once you know your personal why—your purpose—then you can build the type of practice that fulfills your dreams and your clients' needs.

Know and Live by Your Values

Closely aligned with your purpose are your values—the fundamental *beliefs* that guide or motivate your attitude and actions. We recommend identifying your most important values; most advisors have not taken this important step.

At North Star, we use an activity with our advisors called "the values exercise." We learned about this incredibly revealing activity from its co-creator, Doug Lennick, the CEO and cofounder of Think2Perform.[6]

Using a deck of fifty cards with a value and its definition printed on each one, we ask an advisor to select his or her top five values. It is quite difficult to narrow the choices down to five. When you select your top five values, that does not mean you have no regard for the other values; it just means those are your primary values. Some of them can be values we aspire to.

For example, health may be one of my top values, but I may need to become more physically fit. Even though I'm not where I need to be, it is still one of my values. We are constantly striving to realize our values fully.

Once we know your top five values, our ability to coach you in alignment with your values improves considerably. We want what you want. If we know your values, we will understand what is important to you. Once we know those values, we can coach you to make decisions that align with your values and contribute to your getting exactly what you want. We will know what you will and will not agree to. We want you to know *yourself* that well, too—to know what you will and will not agree to, what you will fight for, what motivates you, what defines you. Once you know that, your values

_____

6. Doug Lennick is the CEO and cofounder of Think2Perform. He is legendary for his innovative approaches to developing high performance in individuals and organizations and is an expert at developing practical applications of the art and science of human behavior, financial and otherwise. Before founding Think2Perform, Doug, a CERTIFIED FINANCIAL PLANNER™ professional, was Executive Vice President – Advice and Retail Distribution for American Express Financial Advisors (now Ameriprise Financial). In that role, he led an organization of 17,000 field and corporate associates to unprecedented success.

simply become a matter of execution.

The same is true of your clients. If you know what your clients value in life, you can tailor your financial advice in a way that leads them to achieve and preserve those values.

If we were to look at your calendar, we could determine what your values are. You cannot manage time. We all have the same amount of time; it goes by at the same rate for all of us. But you *can* manage our priorities. Where you spend your time should match your values and reflect who you are as a person. If you leave at two o'clock so that you can be with your daughter at her dental appointment, we already know a lot about you. A Practice on Purpose from a tactical standpoint is that you build your calendar around the priorities you have established.

We coach advisors to build their calendars beginning with setting time aside for their families and time away from the practice to go on vacation and rejuvenate themselves. Certain days of the week are your prep days (typically Monday and Friday), and certain days are your focus days, your high-energy days when you will be more effective with clients (typically Tuesday, Wednesday, and Thursday). Then you decide which clients you are going to see on which days. That is one of the ways you build a Practice on Purpose.

The advisor who comes to work and reacts to new emails, phone calls, and questions is not building a Practice on Purpose. We have advisors who have no pre-booked appointments. They are just showing up. Their clients are driving their practices. They react to the whims of anyone who comes along. They are unable to distinguish between urgent and important matters. They are not happening to the practice; the practice is happening to them.

Stephen Covey, the author of *7 Habits of Highly Effective People*, does an exercise on stage during some of his presentations to demonstrate the importance of prioritizing what's important. He has two big Plexiglass bowls on a table. In one bowl, he places a whole bunch of small beans. Next to that, he has three large rocks.

He gets a participant from the audience and asks her, "What are the most important things in your life?" The participant might say, "Family, faith, and career." He explains to the audience that the beans represent all the little chores in life like getting your laundry done, grocery shopping, paying your taxes, mowing your lawn, and calling your parents.

Then he tells the participant, "I want you to take the three big rocks and put them into the bowl with all the little beans. But you can't have them sticking out over the top of the bowl because the bowl represents the amount of time you have in your life." The participant tries but cannot fit the big rocks in the bowl on top of all the beans.

Next, he has the audience member put the three big rocks into an empty bowl first and then add as many beans as will fit into the bowl. There is enough space between the big rocks that all the beans can fit.

The moral of the story is if you don't take care of the big rocks, or priorities, first, you won't get to them. But if you put the big rocks in first, then you can fit in the little, less important priorities into your life.

The advisor who has a Practice on Purpose takes care of the big priorities first. One of our advisors goes to the gym to work out for an hour before work. Then, for the first four hours of his work day, he is prospecting, calling leads, and marketing. He does the hardest work of his day in the first four hours. Then his day gets easier because he already has the big rocks in place. Your rocks are your values, which become your priorities.

You can ask a hundred different top-performing advisors, managing partners, physicians, attorneys, or anyone else what their values are. And even if they all share a high level of integrity, character, and passion for what they do, they probably have widely varying values.

Phil, Ed, and I have done the values exercise, and there is little overlap among our values:

Gary's Top Five Values

1. Achievement
2. Meaningful work
3. Family
4. Health
5. Leadership

Phil's Top Five Values

1. Religion
2. Family
3. Integrity
4. Independence
5. Leadership

Ed's Top Five Values

1. Integrity
2. Spirituality
3. Loyalty
4. Leadership
5. Excellence

Know Your Personal Brand

Related to knowing and acting on your "why" is the litmus test of your personal brand. Stated briefly, what is the next thought people have when they hear your name? Do they think talented, kind, good-hearted, successful, responsible, a person of integrity? Or do they think difficult, in it for yourself, touchy, egotistical, crabby? It takes years to build your personal brand. It is the sum of all the interactions someone has with you. And it's visceral. It's that quick reaction you form in your head when you hear a person's name.

As we will state numerous times in this book, when you know your purpose, your best years are ahead of you. When you know your "why," know your values, and are deliberate in your behaviors, you will craft your personal brand. It is your superpower, and it must be protected.

 **Discussion Question**

Ask people you trust and respect to share with you what they think is your personal brand. Do you like it? Do you want it to change? Know your personal brand, and describe it in writing.

Lead with Advice, Not Solutions

Our products and services have become more complex than ever. Many of our prospects and even clients don't understand them.

But the basic premise is simple: we want to be financially secure and confident. This is true whether you're an advisor, a client, or anyone else. And that is the reason we have chosen this career—so we can guide our clients to a better outcome. The way we do that is to discover what is important to our clients and then design financial plans that address everything they want, dream of, and need.

To figure this out, we have to ask people questions and guide them in visioning. Too many advisors start out by offering solutions before they even know their clients' financial situations or goals. They begin their meetings by explaining how annuities, life insurance, long-term care, or some other product can benefit them—before those individuals have even discussed what they want and need.

Here is a great set of questions to get your conversations started. The legendary Kinder brothers recommended these questions in their workshops. You simply say to your client, "Imagine you have all the money you will ever need, now and in the future. What will you do with it? How will you live your life? What will change?"

This line of questioning enables you to get to the heart of what's important to each client.

Here are three more questions you can ask to get clients thinking about what's important:

1. If you knew you were dying tomorrow, what decisions would you have to make?
2. If you knew you were going to live for six months, what decisions would you have to make?
3. Or if you had five years to live, what decisions would you make?

Finally, here are four additional questions to ask your clients to discover their priorities:

1. Why are you working so hard?
2. What do you want your money to do for you?
3. What's really important to you about money? What will it enable you to do?
4. What is your money story? When you grew up, how did your parents educate you about money?

Providing ongoing financial advice and partnering with your clients during every step of their financial journey can be the foundation of your practice. After all, the assets themselves aren't what's important to people—they aren't collecting piles of money in a room to admire. They are working hard so they can have life experiences that matter and to increase their confidence about the future.

It's our job to lead clients to discover what their hopes, dreams, concerns, and fears are about money. In the discovery process, we cannot assume clients know what they want. This is why our focus must be on advice, not solutions.

 **Discussion Question**

What specific questions will you ask your clients to get to the heart of what's most important to them? Consider the sample questions just listed, and then decide on those you like the best. Write them down.

A Framing Shift: Creation vs. Competition

Like many other professions, insurance and financial services has traditionally been driven by agents, advisors, companies, firms, and practices competing with one another to claim a bigger slice of the "pie."

Competition is a zero-sum game. It requires that someone wins and someone else has to lose. Competition is a scarcity mentality, as opposed to an abundance mentality. Competing with other advisors all the time is fatiguing and draining. And it's ancient!

There are a lot of financial advisors and firms out there—many different approaches, explanations, and ways of providing financial services. It's a complex and crowded space.

We invite you to seize your unique opportunity to *create* instead of *competing*. When you create an intimate, personal connection with your clients regarding their hopes, dreams, fears, and goals around money, you move *beyond* competition. You become irreplaceable in your clients' hearts and minds. When you connect deeply with your clients about their money and provide advice they can't get anywhere else, *you* are the value. Your commitment, passion, and dedication to leading your clients to financial well-being transcend competition.

This is an incredibly refreshing perspective, and it can change your career, your life, and your clients' lives. It simply requires a mindset shift. It's walking through that archway.

Discussion Question

When you create intimate, personal connections with clients regarding their hopes, dreams, fears, and goals around money, you move *beyond* competition. You become irreplaceable in your clients' hearts and minds. What are some specific actions you can take to connect deeply with your clients? What will you do from now on to let your clients know you're thinking about them between meetings?

Today there are companies like Starbucks and Apple that are exceptionally successful. People don't know how they would function without the products and value propositions these companies seemingly invented out of thin air.

I have an iPhone, and I can't leave the house without it. But I didn't have one ten years ago. Similarly, a lot of people can't start their day without stopping by Starbucks. How did that happen? That's how we want you to think about being a financial advisor—your clients cannot do without you.

A Note About the "Real" Competition

The only real competition in our business is the threat of *death, old age, illness, and poverty*—and we are in a race to get to our clients before our "competition" does. Death comes for all of us— and old age, illness, and poverty will come for many. This is the real competition for financial advisors and firms.

We must have those tough conversations about securing the future with our clients, without hesitation—and early, when they can better protect their financial future.

We serve our clients in the best way possible when we elevate our profession beyond competition and focus instead on creating unique value.

Become Indispensable to Your Clients: The Oatmeal Story

I like to tell the oatmeal story. It demonstrates how advisors become indispensable and irreplaceable to their clients once they build that trusted relationship.

An advisor I know named Jane had to increase her planning fees at a certain point in her career. She had not done so in five years. She told one of her clients she needed to increase her fee, and the client asked her why. Jane explained to the client that her financial plan had grown in complexity, which required more of Jane's time.

The client said, "Jane, I want you to know something. I would eat oatmeal for dinner every day of the week to save enough money to pay your fee. That's how important you are to our family."

Remember this story if you ever get bogged down in the mechanics of our business—all the ways in which investments function, the cost of investments, life insurance complexity, annuity strategy, etc. Advisors have to understand a ton of products, services, and concepts. But it's all bland and meaningless until you couple that technical knowledge with true compassion for your clients' hopes, fears, and dreams around money.

"Can I Step Out of the Workforce?"

What good is having assets if clients are working themselves until death?

Erik is one of our advisors at North Star, and he loves financial planning. Among his clients are a married couple who are both doctors.

One day, the doctors were describing their life goals to Erik. One of the doctors wanted to know if she could stop working because they had two young children at home. Both parents were struggling to keep up with their careers while also making sure their children were making academic progress at school. They both worked long hours and felt guilty that they weren't spending more time with their children.

They were driving themselves into the ground. Not even the core values that had initially energized their careers could lead them to overcome the stress they were experiencing. They knew that if they were working so hard that their kids might not have a warm and nurturing upbringing, what good was the money?

The mom asked Erik, "Can I step out of the workforce?"

He analyzed their situation, based on her question. Erik did the analysis and told her, "Great news! You can stop working until both of your kids graduate from high school. Then you can re-establish your practice if you want to. But even if you don't, you both will be OK financially."

Erik said he could sense the immense relief both of his clients felt. Suddenly, they saw hope. They saw that, because of planning and working with a trustworthy advisor, they could find a way to achieve what mattered the most to them.

Focusing on Financial Advice Increases Your Value to Clients

One reason why advisors' focus on AUM diminished in recent years is the commoditization of products leveled the playing field.

Even as far back as 2015, a Deloitte study found the basis for competition among advisors had changed. Advisors focused on their clients' investment activities such as portfolio allocation, stock picking, and mutual fund selection. That focus required them to try to convince clients of their ability to deliver superior investment returns for them. But most wealth-management firms had access to basically the same products, tools, and models.

Just as important, advisors focusing on AUM failed to generate above-market average returns for their clients. One study, published by the National Bureau of Economic Research, found that investors who worked with an advisor gained around 1.8 percent per year. But those investors were paying, on average, an additional 1.7 percent for that advisor, which canceled out nearly all the additional return. That made it difficult for most financial advisors to demonstrate their value to clients.[7]

The 2015 Deloitte study concluded, "To meet investor needs, wealth-management firms and their advisors should shift to holistic, goals-based advice and measure performance based on achieving clients' goals within agreed time frames rather than beating market benchmarks. This is also a way to broaden the range of advice advisors provide, from investment to wealth management, and escape the commoditization of investment advice."[8]

Because advisors generally have been unable to consistently deliver exceptional value in managing clients' assets, that focus is no longer viable. But financial advice holds exceptional promise for a robust, successful practice.

You Will Serve a Broader Clientele

Now, even if we *were* worried about competition from other advisors and firms, statistics tell us that there is more than enough

7. "10 Disruptive Trends in Wealth Management," Deloitte, 2015, https://www2.deloitte.com/content/dam/Deloitte/us/Documents/strategy/us-cons-disruptors-in-wealth-mgmt-final.pdf.
8. Ibid.

business for everyone.

One obvious reason is that a focus on AUM limits advisors to clientele who have considerable enough assets to manage. But once you change your focus to providing financial advice, you will have a much broader reach. There is unlimited business out there, for several reasons. Here are three.

1. Only 30 Percent of Consumers Have Advisors

A 2021 survey revealed that only 30 percent of consumers have a paid financial advisor.[9] This fact alone points to the ample opportunities out there—70 percent of consumers do not have advisors!

The COVID-19 pandemic created increased interest in working with advisors. Surveys taken during the pandemic revealed that 30 percent of consumers without financial advisors said they planned to actively seek one in the next year.[10]

2. The Pandemic Created a Huge Demand for Financial Advice, Especially Among Millennials

The pandemic created an acute awareness among Millennials (those born between 1981 and 1996) to plan for the future. After surviving the economic downturn of 2008, the pandemic that wreaked havoc on the world beginning in 2020 gave them another wake-up call.

The growing demand to provide financial advice to Millennials presents you with an unprecedented opportunity.

The sixth annual "Advisor Authority" study from the Nationwide

9. "Half of Consumers Think Financial Advisors Are More Expensive Than They Are, But Almost All Who Use One Say They're Worth It," Devon Delfino, MagnifyMoney, last updated on March 22, 2021, https://www.magnifymoney.com/blog/news/financial-advisors-cost-survey/#ConsumersKeyfindings.
10. "Women as the Next Wave of Growth in US Wealth Management," Pooneh Baghai, Olivia Howard, Lakshmi Prakash, and Jill Zucker, McKinsey & Company, July 29, 2020, https://www.mckinsey.com/industries/financial-services/our-insights/women-as-the-next-wave-of-growth-in-us-wealth-management.

Retirement Institute® reported that in 2016, 50 percent of Millennials said they had an advisor. By 2020, that number had grown to 75 percent. This generation, representing one-third of the entire US population, is extremely tuned in with the need for careful planning. In this study, 84 percent of Millennials acknowledged that they could do all the right things to manage their finances and still be blindsided by outside events.[11]

That is the type of clients we want to save—those who understand the value of financial advice.

3. More Women Are Seeking Financial Advice

Women are, and have always been, underrepresented in financial services—both in terms of the number of women advisors and the number of women clients. There aren't enough advisors to serve the majority of our population.

McKinsey reports that, compared with five years ago, 30 percent more married women are making financial and investment decisions. And more women than ever are the family breadwinners, spurring growth in their investable assets. Also, an unprecedented amount of assets will shift into the hands of US women over the next three to five years. This shift represents a $30 trillion opportunity by the end of the decade. Women are more likely than men to feel they have a critical gap in meeting their key financial goals. This is especially true for widows; 70 percent of women switch their wealth relationship to a new financial institution within a year of their spouse's death.[12]

The McKinsey study also found that women are more willing to pay a premium for in-person financial advice than men are. Many

---

11. "Millennials Defying Financial Stereotypes, Survey Finds," Alan Goforth, April 23, 2021, *ThinkAdvisor*, https://www.thinkadvisor.com/2021/04/23/millennials-defying-financial-stereotypes-survey-finds-415-408031/.

12. "Women as the Next Wave of Growth in US Wealth Management," Pooneh Baghai, Olivia Howard, Lakshmi Prakash, and Jill Zucker, McKinsey & Company, July 29, 2020, https://www.mckinsey.com/industries/financial-services/our-insights/women-as-the-next-wave-of-growth-in-us-wealth-management.

place a high value on establishing a personal connection with their advisors. Roughly a third of affluent women say they would only work with an investment professional they trust, roughly ten percentage points more than men.[13]

One might ask, "Do women intuitively discern the *trustworthy* advisor versus the trusted—but ultimately unscrupulous—advisor such as Bernie Madoff?" You see, Bernie Madoff was a *trusted* advisor, which is why he was able to embezzle $60 billion from his clients. But he was not a *trustworthy* advisor, as they later learned. A *trusted* advisor is what others think you are; a *trustworthy* advisor is what you really are!

And often, the advisors people trust are women. Yet in early 2021, women represented only 18.1 percent of total financial advisor head count, up from 15.7 percent in 2015.[14]

We have a moral purpose to include everyone—men, women, and people of various racial and ethnic groups—in the journey toward realizing financial security.

There are ample opportunities to serve women consumers.

Analysis by McKinsey's PriceMetrix indicates that simply by retaining Baby Boomer clients, firms could see one-third higher revenue potential. And firms that acquire and retain younger women—especially Millennials—as clients could see up to four times faster revenue growth.[15]

Do some quick calculations. Do you see how your practice could change for the better with one-third higher revenue and up to four times faster revenue growth?

---

13. Ibid.
14. "Women, People of Color Still Vastly Underrepresented Among Financial Advisors," Jacqueline Sergeant, *Financial Advisor*, January 14, 2021, https://www.fa-mag.com/news/women-and-people-of-color-still-vastly-underrepresented-among-financial-advisors-59778.html.
15. Ibid.

Advice-Seeking Millennials Care About Your Values

Earlier, we mentioned that Millennials, especially, are seeking financial advice. They recognize the incomparable value of planning ahead.

Another characteristic that is rather unique to Millennials is that they care about what you believe in and stand for.

Ben Harrison of BNY Mellon's Pershing, whom we mentioned earlier, says the COVID-19 pandemic created a sense of urgency about planning for the future among many people, notably Millennials.

"A growing number of self-directed, first-time investors are entering the market with the hopes of putting their assets—and time—to work and getting an early start in the investing world," Harrison writes. "Meanwhile, the oldest Millennials are reaching their 40s, entering an era of critical life decisions. Having already gone through two recessions, anxiety runs high among this group of investors, who are increasingly turning to professional help to manage their finances."[16]

Harrison notes that Millennials have different expectations than previous generations. "Millennials don't want to be just sold services," he says. "They want to know what you stand for. In fact, a whopping 83 percent of Millennials say they would be more loyal to a company that helps them contribute to social and environmental issues. To appeal to this group, advisors need to be clear about their personal brand, purpose, and values, as well as differentiators. They must live and breathe those values at every client touch point—on and offline."[17]

I want to repeat one of his statements because it is important: "Advisors need to be clear about their personal brand, purpose, and values, as well as differentiators."

---

16. "Op-Ed: There's an Increased Demand for Financial Advice. Are Advisors Up to the Challenge?" Ben Harrison, CNBC, March 22 20218, https://www.cnbc.com/2021/03/22/can-advisors-meet-the-ever-increasing-demand-for-financial-advice.html.
17. Ibid.

The World Needs You: Many Prospects, Too Few Advisors

As mentioned, our profession is experiencing an unprecedented oversupply of prospects and undersupply of advisors. First, consider these numbers, which demonstrate the seemingly endless opportunities we have to serve clients.

Oversupply of Prospects:

- From 2021 to 2030, 10,000 Baby Boomers (people born between 1946 and 1964) will reach retirement age every day.[18]

- The average 401(k) balance for Americans between the ages of 40 and 49 was $120,800, as of the fourth quarter of 2020.[19]

- Of the 47.8 million Americans ages 65 and older, the average income is only $38,515, according to the US Census Bureau, and their average net worth is $170,516.[20]

- Because of the COVID-19 pandemic, 67 percent of people surveyed in February 2021 said they planned to retire later than originally planned.[21]

- Only 33 percent of Americans have a long-term financial plan.[22]

---

18. "The Baby Boomer Generation," Jeff Hoyt, SeniorLiving.org, updated August 9, 2021, https://www.seniorliving.org/life/baby-boomers/.

19. "Here's How Much Money Americans in Their 40's Have in Their 401(k) Accounts," Nadine El-Bawab, CNBC, April 1, 2021, https://www.cnbc.com/2021/04/01/how-much-americans-in-their-40s-have-in-their-401k-accounts.html.

20. "Jaw-Dropping Stats About the State of Retirement in America," Jordan Rosenfeld, GoBankingRates.com, September 16, 2021, https://www.gobankingrates.com/retirement/planning/jaw-dropping-stats-state-retirement-america/.

21. "Retirement Insecurity 2021: Americans' Views of Retirement," Tyler Bond, Dan Doonan, and Kelly Kenneally, National Institute on Retirement Security, February 2021, https://www.nirsonline.org/wp-content/uploads/2021/02/FINAL-Retirement-Insecurity-2021-.pdf.

22. "2021 State of Retirement Planning Study," Fidelity Investments, 2021, https://s2.q4cdn.com/997146844/files/doc_news/2021/03/24/State-of-Retirement-Planning_Fact-Sheet_FINAL.pdf.

- As a result of the financial upheavals caused by the COVID-19 pandemic, 38 percent of survey respondents said they were working with a financial advisor in August 2021, up from 29 percent who worked with one before the pandemic. Another 15 percent of respondents did not have an advisor before the pandemic but were planning to work with one in the future.[23]

Undersupply of advisors:

As our aging advisor population begins to retire, too few young people are entering our profession to replace them. This is one reason why North Star Resource Group has focused on hiring talent on college campuses for many years. We need an infusion of youth in our profession—and we have for a long time.

Additionally, we hire for character and train for competence, which preserves our culture.

The following statistics demonstrate the dire need in this country for financial advisors who provide clients with priceless advice, wisdom, discipline, and compassion:

- As of 2019, the number of financial advisors had not grown or shrunk by more than 1 percent since a 3 percent decline in 2012. The advisor population is expected to shrink even more because of the impending retirement of many advisors, according to a 2020 report by Cerulli Associates. The firm reports that over the next ten years, more than 111,500 advisors will retire. Those advisors represent more than one-third of the workforce and assets in the United States.[24]

23. "Americans Are Changing Who They Turn to for Financial Advice," Francisco Velasquez, CNBC, August 28, 2021, https://www.cnbc.com/2021/08/28/americans-are-changing-who-they-turn-to-for-financial-advice.html.

24. "The Wave of Advisor Retirements Is About to Break," Michael Thrasher, RIAIntel, February 5, 2020, https://www.riaintel.com/article/b1k6vknndm4grt/the-wave-of-advisor-retirements-is-about-to-break.

- The average age of financial advisors is the mid-fifties, and many are in their sixties and seventies. Studies show that most small practices—particularly solo practitioners—have no successor to fill their shoes.[25]

- In 2020, women represented only 18.1 percent of the total financial advisor head count.[26] As we have noted, women clients are five times more likely to prefer a female advisor.

- Women are more likely than men to feel they have a critical gap in meeting their key financial goals. This is especially true for widows: as mentioned, 70 percent of women switch their wealth relationship to a new financial institution within a year of their spouse's death.[27]

- By 2030, American women are expected to control much of the $30 trillion in financial assets that Baby Boomers will possess—a potential wealth transfer of such magnitude that it approaches the annual GDP of the United States.[28]

There has been no better time in history to be a financial advisor than now—and to transition to an advice-based model in your practice.

25. "As Advisors Start to 'Age Out,' Firms Look to Step Up Succession Planning," Andrew Osterland, CNBC, updated October 19, 2019, https://www.cnbc.com/2019/10/29/financial-advisors-need-succession-plan-to-benefit-clients-and-firm.html.
26. "Parity Is an Uphill Climb for Women and BIPOC Financial Advisors," Cerulli Associates, January 14, 2021, https://www.cerulli.com/news/parity-is-an-uphill-climb-for-women-and-bipoc-financial-advisors.
27. "Women as the Next Wave of Growth in US Wealth Management," McKinsey & Company, July 29, 2020, https://www.mckinsey.com/industries/financial-services/our-insights/women-as-the-next-wave-of-growth-in-us-wealth-management.
28. Ibid.

Discussion Question

Go back and read the McKinsey prediction about the future of this profession again. To what extent do you agree or disagree with the research firm's statement that in the next decade, advisors will "gradually shed their role as investment managers and become more like integrated life/wealth coaches who advise clients on investments, banking, health care, protection, taxes, estate, and financial wellness needs more broadly"?

You Are Among the Most Esteemed Professionals

As a financial advisor who knows and lives out your purpose daily, you are making a lasting positive impact in your clients' lives.

Your value is so great, in fact, that we believe you are in the same esteemed category as airline pilots, surgeons, and members of the clergy.

Airline pilots make it possible for people to travel the world in a fraction of time it took before we had airplanes. Surgeons save people's lives. Members of the clergy lead people to spiritual fulfillment. And advisors enable people to live their best lives possible with the money they have.

Please never doubt the influence you have on your clients' lives.

We want you to think of yourself as being a combination of a life coach and a financial coach. What a great way to make an impact! Short of a surgeon or clergy person, who else but you, a financial advisor, can make that kind of impact on a household and the many generations that follow? Always remember that the Miracle of Life Insurance enables you to change the lives of client descendants a hundred years from now and that they will never know your name, but your selfless Practice on Purpose attitude cares not.

The Intersection of Health, Wealth, and Happiness

Your advice, tailored to your clients' individual situations, can lead them to the blissful intersection of health, wealth, and happiness.

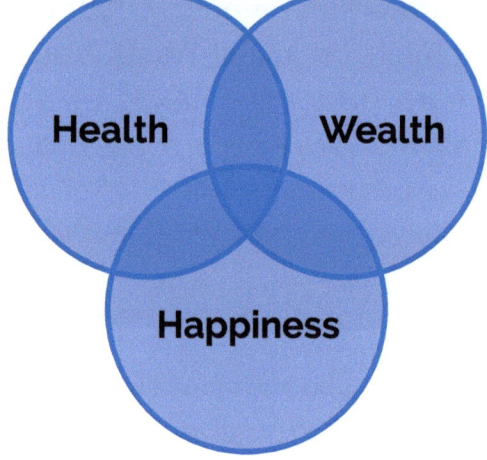

We believe this fully. It's also the focus of a great book titled *Leveraging Your Financial Intelligence: At the Intersection of Money, Health, and Happiness* by Douglas Lennick, Roy Geer, and Ryan Goulart.

The authors write that approximately 90 percent of all people are stressed about money and that stress takes its toll on every part of their lives. They say financial health, physical health, and happiness are so profoundly interconnected that it's almost impossible to enjoy any one of these without the help of the other two. They describe this phenomenon as "the intersection of money, health, and happiness." As you take steps to improve your financial well-being, they say, you will discover that leveraging your financial intelligence will also fuel your physical and emotional well-being.[29]

Now, let's look at these three aspects of people's overall well-being in more detail.

1. Health

Worrying about finances can lead to a variety of problems.

Early in 2020, Capital One published its Mind Over Money Study. This was before the COVID-19 pandemic wreaked havoc on the economy and on people's personal financial situations. The study revealed that 77 percent of Americans felt anxious about their personal financial situations. Also, stress related to financial issues caused 45 percent of the survey respondents to feel fatigued, 42 percent to have difficulty concentrating at work, and 41 percent to experience sleep problems.[30]

Companies reported that employees with high financial stress were twice as likely to report poor health overall and were more than four times as likely to complain of headaches, depression, or other ailments.

Researchers found a simple but effective solution. They found that getting people to *focus on a bigger-picture view of their finances*, as opposed to focusing on small details, can help reduce the stress they experienced as a result of their financial situations. Research showed that thinking about long-term goals, even for a few seconds, can help mitigate the negative effects of stress on financial decision making. Individuals who think more about the big picture are more likely to feel in control of their lives and finances, more likely to have a written budget, and less likely to spend their total paycheck as soon as they get it.

Now, who is uniquely qualified to encourage people to focus on

29. Douglas Lennick, Roy Geer, and Ryan Goulart, *Leveraging Your Financial Intelligence: At the Intersection of Money, Health, and Happiness* (Hoboken, New Jersey: John Wiley & Sons, Inc., 2018).

30. "Does Stress Have a Negative Impact on Your Financial Decisions? You're Not Alone," Herb Weisbaum, NBC News, February 3, 2020, https://www.nbcnews.com/better/lifestyle/does-stress-have-negative-impact-your-financial-decisions-you-re-ncna1128951.

their long-term financial goals? *You* are. You are the product. You are the value. Your advice is priceless.

2. Wealth

Research consistently shows that people who work with financial advisors tend to have better financial outcomes than those who don't. Statistics on this topic are scarce, but it's important to consider the overall value of working with a financial advisor—not just the growth in your portfolio.

A capable advisor will guide clients in setting specific goals, setting and following a budget, avoiding the temptation to react emotionally to market downturns, customizing their financial plans, and then adjusting them as needed. These are all critical components of building, growing, and preserving wealth.

3. Happiness

In 2019, Northwestern Mutual released its tenth Planning and Progress Study, which revealed that 92 percent of people say nothing makes them happier or more confident in life than having their financial house in order. While only about one-third of the survey respondents said they have worked with a financial advisor, those who do so report much greater financial stability. Also, 66 percent of the survey respondents who had a financial advisor said they felt financially secure, compared to 30 percent of those who were not paying for professional help.[31]

Your unique opportunity is to create an intimate personal connection with your clients around their hopes, dreams, and fears about money. When you make that kind of a connection, you are irreplaceable. There is no competition from other advisors, whether robo or breathing. You become uniquely positioned to guide your

---

31. "People with a Financial Advisor Say They Aren't Just Better with Money—They're Happier with Life Overall," Tanza Loudenback, *Business Insider,* July 24, 2019, https://www.businessinsider.com/personal-finance/financial-advisor-worth-the-cost-for-money-advice-2019-7.

clients in living their best possible lives.

Financial advice is about goal achievement, but it's also about navigating the complexities and uncertainties of life. It's not only about financial health; it's about financial wellness and how expert financial advice makes all our lives better. When people are financially healthy, other areas of their lives improve. They become happier.

They feel like they have more choices. They begin to replace that worry about having enough money in retirement with excitement about the possibilities in their future.

 **Discussion Question**

Stop here, and paraphrase what it means to you to guide your clients by leading them to the intersection of health, wealth, and happiness. It is important for you to say these concepts out loud, in addition to reading them.

Advisors' Biggest Obstacle: The Elephant and the Stake

Given the compelling reasons we've discussed for transitioning to an advice-based practice, and to charge appropriately for the value you provide, it seems to be an obvious choice. Yet many advisors have a difficult time charging what they're worth. Why is that?

At North Star, one of our primary sources of new talent is hiring brand-new people from college campuses. The advantages of this strategy are limitless. They tend to fit well into our culture and are open to adopting and respecting our values. They generally go with the flow. They are like the liquid that takes the shape of whatever vessel it's poured into. If you pour it into a flask, it looks like a flask. If you pour it into a cup, it looks like a cup.

The biggest disadvantage is the enormity of capital needed to hire and train twenty-two-year-olds from college campuses. A second disadvantage is that, for the first two to four years of their careers, nobody wants to talk to them. That's not good for their self-esteem. It makes them feel like their knowledge is not valuable. It's difficult for them to overcome that mindset.

Even after they get five or ten years of experience, many of them *still* don't know how to charge for their valuable advice because they never learned how to do so. Phil compares this situation to a baby elephant tied to a stake—he isn't strong enough to pull the stake out of the ground, so he stops trying. When he gets to be a big elephant, he could easily pull the stake out because it's the same stake that's always been there, and he is now much bigger and stronger. But his mind has been hardwired to think he can't pull the stake out of the ground, so he gives up.

Many new advisors have a similar mindset.

Many of the thirty-two-year-olds who started out in this business ten years earlier have a hard time telling a client, "The advice needed to answer your question is four thousand dollars. That's how much I'm going to charge you for my time." They're still tied to the stake. They still have the perception that nobody wants to talk to them, and nobody wants their advice. It creates an uphill battle when we are trying to develop advisors and coach them to provide clients with optimum service. Even after years of experience and obtaining hard-earned designations such as the CLU® and the ChFC®, many advisors struggle with their ability to charge for their valuable advice.

Firms that hire career changers don't tend to have this problem because they often hire people who have been in positions in which they were comfortable with charging an appropriate fee for their education, credentials, knowledge, wisdom, and experience.

For some reason, it's different for attorneys. An attorney who has just graduated from law school and gets hired into a firm might make $50 or $100 an hour. The law firm's partners who are making $400 an hour have set that rate for the new attorney, who doesn't have a problem with that. But for some reason, what is so natural for an attorney is unnatural for somebody who comes into the financial services business, especially at a young age.

Once we recognized this uphill battle years ago, we began to address the issue in our advisor-development process. As a result, the number of families who are in ongoing advice relationships with advisors at North Star increased dramatically. We achieved that increase one advisor at a time. We counseled advisors individually in weekly or biweekly meetings.

Everyone benefits when advisors engage in ongoing advice relationships—the firm, the advisors, and especially the clients. To build an effective Practice on Purpose based on ongoing advice requires a compelling purpose. In chapter 2, we explore how to discover your purpose and to design your practice around it.

 **Discussion Question**

Have you known any advisors who were like the elephant at the stake—unaware of their ability to break free from old obstacles? Have you experienced this limiting mindset yourself? Explain what it means to you to move beyond this mindset and to charge what your advice is worth.

CHAPTER 2

DISCOVERING YOUR PURPOSE

Most people know about the ship named *Titanic* that sank on the night of Sunday, April 15th, 1912. What most people don't know is that another ship called the *Carpathia* was 58 miles away at the time. Other ships were closer to the *Titanic*, but they did not have on their radios. Marconi wireless radios were just becoming required equipment. The *Carpathia* still had its radio on, and the crew heard the distress signal come across the airwaves. It was the only ship to pick up that signal.

They knew the *Titanic* was in trouble and that they had to get to it—fast.

The crew headed toward the *Titanic*. They began burning deck chairs and other furniture in the boilers so the ship would weigh less and travel faster. They had a clear purpose: the only thing that mattered at that moment was to get to the *Titanic* and try to save lives.

They steamed through the night, all night, without sleeping. They were *all in*. By the time they reached the *Titanic*, it had already sunk. People were in the water, struggling to stay afloat and avoid hypothermia. The *Carpathia* crew put every life preserver and boat they had into the water, to try to save lives.

Every life preserver saved a life. Advisors do the same.

They had clarity of purpose. There was no distraction. There was no fuzziness, no ambiguity. They knew what they had to do.

Clarity of purpose is an important part of thriving and evolving as a financial advisor. Financial advisors who have a clear purpose in their work will be better equipped to provide an exceptional client experience.

Also, the stronger your sense of purpose is, the better able you are to create *your* best life possible.

Clarity of Purpose: The Rescue of a Soccer Team from a Cave in Thailand

A more recent true-life story that demonstrates the power of clarity of purpose is that of the rescue of a group of boys who got trapped in a cave in Thailand by torrential rain.

On June 23, 2018, twelve members of the Wild Boars soccer team and their coach entered caves in Northern Thailand to perform a ceremony. Heavy rainfall began, causing flooding that trapped them all in the Tham Luang Nang Non cave system.

Hundreds of rescuers from around the world teamed up to rescue the boys. It took nine days for the divers to find the boys and their coach, huddled together above the lapping water, 2.5 miles from the cave's entrance. It took another eight days to rescue them all. The boys and their coach survived with little food and water in the flooded cave during the seventeen days they were trapped.[32]

It would be easy to give up in a situation like that. But they didn't lose hope during the complicated rescue.

Divers and medical professionals stayed with the boys and delivered medicine and food to increase their strength. The boys had to learn how to swim and dive before they could start their journey out of the cave. Swim lessons are rare in Thailand, where drowning is the leading cause of death for children under the age of fifteen. It took several days to bring all thirteen people out of the cave.[33]

The coach and all twelve boys survived because of their own determination and because of the unified effort of people from all over the world to rescue them. Everyone involved had clarity of purpose. They worked together toward a singular mission. That

32. "This Timeline Shows Exactly How the Thai Cave Rescue Unfolded and What's Happened Since," Pat Ralph and James Pasley, *Business Insider*, updated June 24, 2019, https://www.businessinsider.com/thai-cave-rescue-timeline-how-it-unfolded-2018-7.
33. Ibid.

type of commitment, resolve, and purpose builds strength and force when many people share it.

This story punctuates the important role we all play in guiding clients to financial security and prosperity. This is why it is important to define, and be clear about, the purpose of your financial practice.

What Is the Purpose of Your Financial Practice?

Many people have no idea what their *why* is. When we coach advisors, it often takes two or three meetings to bring it to the surface. Once they connect with their *why*, they get clear about their purpose. And it changes their practices for the better—dramatically.

We want to challenge you to identify what is your *why*. You can borrow someone else's compelling story if you don't have a strong one of your own. This business is too important not to have a compelling *why*. And frankly, serving your clients without clarity of purpose makes this job harder.

Our friend Mark Twain said, "The two most important days of your life are the day you were born and the day you find out why." We believe that.

Isn't this a refreshing revelation? No matter how long you've been in the profession, there's more good stuff ahead of you. You always want to have something bigger and better in front of you than behind you. It makes life a lot better, doesn't it?

A professor once told me, "Once you state your intention to the public, it takes on its own form. It will come and find you."

When you write down your purpose, it's almost like a proclamation of faith.

It's more difficult to write than you might think, but once you do it, it's quite therapeutic and meaningful. When you write out your purpose and then share it with someone else, it's revealing, and you might feel vulnerable. But once you state it in front of other people, now it's public, and you have to live by it.

Brazilian author Paulo Coelho wrote, "When you want something, all the universe conspires in helping you to achieve it." The world works in ways we don't completely understand. When you state your purpose and vision and set out to achieve it, the world collaborates with you to make it come true.

As you decide how to define and describe the purpose of your practice, I thought it might be helpful for you to read an example. My purpose is as follows:

> To learn and grow as a person so I can change the lives of others through wisdom, advice, vision, and challenges. I strive to love, protect, and lead myself and my family to be the best version of ourselves. I want to live large, be engaged, and discipline myself to add more years to my life and more life in my years.

That might sound like a simple statement, but it took a long time for me to write it. I had to think about it a lot to craft it. But once I wrote it, it was transformational. It became *me*. Some days when I get to the office, I'm not super-motivated. That's why I have my purpose displayed prominently, where I can see it. When I read my purpose, I get motivated and inspired because I want to live up to it.

When you know what your purpose is and what you're striving to achieve, you become laser-focused. We have heard advisors share many compelling stories about how, once they got clear about their purpose and vision, they changed clients' lives and prevented them from making costly mistakes.

If you don't think you offer significant value to changing your clients' financial behavior and outcomes, how can you charge for your advice? On the flip side, once you do acknowledge your value, and you see how your advice changes people's lives, it will inspire you to do more of that.

You Must Have a Strong *Why*—Clarity of Purpose— To Charge for Your Advice

Why are you in this business? Why did you choose this profession? What is your purpose?

To charge for your financial advice, you must first define your *clarity of purpose* as a financial advisor—to figure out your *why*.

Our calling as financial advisors is to save financial lives and produce peace of mind.

 **Discussion Question**

What is your purpose as a financial advisor? What do you hope to accomplish for your clients? What is your compelling and unique offering to them? Write down your purpose. Once you are happy with it, communicate it with your staff and your clients often.

We could tell stories all day about advisors whose clarity of purpose propelled them to success. We will tell you a few of our favorites.

One North Star advisor said that when his father died, there was a $75,000 life insurance policy. His mom took the $75,000, paid off a few credit cards, and went out and bought a brand-new Camaro. He did not know until years later that, at that time, they were behind on their rent and were on food stamps. This advisor said, "I grew up in a really tough situation, and I don't want my clients to go through that."

Another advisor had a brother with Down syndrome. Their parents were older and in declining health. He wanted his brother to be taken care of. He set up a trust so his brother could live in a home that provides quality care. His purpose was to take care of his family.

Still another advisor, Tom, was an advisor in my (Gary's) group. One night, as I was driving home from an event, I drove by his office building. He had a first-floor office in a suburb. I could see him in the office, working. I parked my car, got out, walked up to his office window, and tapped on it. It scared the heck out of hm. He motioned for me to go inside, so I did.

He went to his dorm-sized refrigerator, took out a couple of beers, and we sat down to have a good chat. I said, "Hey, Tom, what are you doing here so late?"

He replied, "Well, it's kind of personal."

"Tell me about it."

He said, "Well, when I was a little kid, I grew up on a farm in west central Minnesota. When I was about fifteen years old, my dad was out plowing the fields late in the day. His tractor tipped over, and he fell underneath it. He died. It was really tough on our family, and I had three younger brothers. For a while, things were pretty good. People would bring over meals. The neighbors came and helped us get the crops in that fall. But as time went on, not many people showed up anymore. I was watching my mom. When we would get home from school, we would go out and do chores. When we came back inside, she had dinner ready for us. I wondered why she didn't eat with us all the time. I finally figured out that there wasn't enough food for all of us. That was a sobering reality. Eventually, she remarried, and things got better, but boy, there was a stretch there that was pretty tough."

Tom shook his head and said, "None of my clients are going to go through that. I will not allow another family to go through what our family went through. The way our family struggled after our dad's accident was 100 percent avoidable, and it caused trauma to us kids, and of course our mom. *That's* why I'm working after seven o'clock tonight."

It was one of the most compelling stories we've ever heard about why an advisor got into this profession. It shows how a compelling purpose inspired him to guide his clients to financial health.

As an advisor, you are saving financial lives.

Identify Your Client Advocates

The amount of revenue clients bring you is not necessarily an indication of who your most valuable clients are. Some of your most valuable clients are those who are *advocates* for you and your practice. They value your service, recommend you to the people they know, and speak highly of you consistently

We do an exercise with advisors in which we look at their top fifty clients—one at a time—to determine how the advisor came to know them. It is a meticulous process. I ask the advisor, "How did you meet that client?" We identify the sources of all fifty clients— were they a recommendation, and if so, who recommended them to the advisor? Did the advisor meet the client at a seminar? Did he or she acquire that client from a purchased list? What happened? What caused that client to join the practice?

In the process of doing that, we start seeing themes. It is often an awakening for you to see the sources of your top fifty clients— the most important people in your practice. If they are almost all from recommendations, the moral of the story is that you probably should get even better at asking for recommendations. Advisors tend to get more clients using that approach than they do by purchasing a list or meeting people at seminars or dinners.

When we realize that one or two clients referred people they know to the advisor, I will circle those clients' names and then draw lines to the names of people they referred to the advisor. I call that the "spider diagram" because at some point, it begins to look like a spider web.

Usually, an advisor's top fifty clients are at the top because of the amount of assets they have invested or the amount of revenue they generate for the advisor. However, I often challenge advisors to rethink their definition of who their top clients are. A client who recommends three or more people to the advisor over the years is a valuable client, even if he or she may not have the amount of assets or income another client has.

That client is an *advocate* for your practice and should be treated as a top-tier client.

Discussion Question

Who are your client advocates? If you have not identified them, list some of them now. Later, go back through your client database and list everyone you consider to be your advocate. What can you do to cultivate these valuable relationships and let these clients know you appreciate them?

Lead Your Clients to Discover *Their* Purpose

Jack Chain was a four-star general in the US military. When he was serving at the Pentagon, which is the foremost military facility in America, as an officer, his ten-year-old daughter asked him, "Hey, Daddy, what do you do for your job?"

His response was, "I answer questions. That's what I do, sweetie. I answer questions."

A couple of years later, he got promoted to commander inside the Pentagon. His daughter asked him again, "Daddy, what is it that you do?"

He said, "I now *ask* the questions."

Leadership isn't so much about *answering* questions; it has a lot more to do with *asking* questions—the right questions.

The first question we need to be asking ourselves is, "What is *my* purpose?" And the question we need to ask our clients is, "What is *your* purpose?"

We all need to know why we're working so hard in life. What are we seeking? What do we want? What are our values and goals? What are we trying to accomplish in this incredible gift of life we've been given?

It is critical that we, as advisors, ask ourselves these questions and come up with meaningful answers that will serve as our road map for the future. It's also critical that we ask our clients these questions. It is important for them, and you, to understand what they are trying to achieve—and why. We recommended some specific questions to ask clients earlier in the book.

Once we have a good understanding of what our clients are striving for, we can begin to guide them toward accomplishing those things. Our advice serves as their road map to the future.

If we don't know what someone wants to accomplish, how can we be a good resource for them?

We've all had clients who want to make knee-jerk, emotional decisions about their money when the market and economy fluctuate. We also know that's a losing proposition—always. Many people panicked during the COVID-19 pandemic. If you kept your clients in the market from January 2020 through mid-2021, and convinced them not to bail out, they are thanking you now.

Along the way, you have guided your clients to know what their purpose is—why they are working so hard to save for the future. And when market upheavals and life transitions happen, you remind them about that purpose and encourage them to stay the course. This is how you change lives, forever.

When You Know Your Purpose, Your Best Years Are Always Ahead of You

This is not a dress rehearsal. This is your real life. It's so much more fun when you have clarity of purpose. This is true for both advisors and consumers. It makes it easier to navigate pandemics and tough economies.

When we take on all the angst of our clients, it can get heavy. It's like a doctor listening all day to people describe being sick. If you don't have a sense of purpose, a strong sense of why you're doing this, you can get beaten down. You can get discouraged. Then you might not give your clients your best advice.

But with a strong sense of purpose, you will be excited about the noble work you do, and you will get your clients excited about their own lives. The future will look bright.

Now, this next sentence is important. It's not just the punch line to this chapter; it's the punch line to this entire book, so we are going to make it stand out:

If you do not have a strong sense of purpose,
it will be hard for you to have the courage
to charge for your advice.

Discussion Question

Let's say a client asks you, "How are you different from other advisors?" You share your purpose with your client, but he or she asks for more details. What will you say? Practice describing your unique value—your Practice on Purpose—until you can say it with complete conviction and confidence.

No matter how long you've been in the profession, your best years are always ahead of you.

CHAPTER 3

ACHIEVING THE PRACTICE YOU DESIRE

When you have a clear understanding of your purpose—why you work hard for your clients—you will value your financial advice and charge appropriately for it. Once you acknowledge your value in your clients' eyes, that realization is likely to supercharge your enthusiasm. You will get up every day wondering, "Who do I *get* to meet with today?" (Not "Who do I *have* to meet with today?")

In turn, your clients will appreciate your passion for helping them, and they will refer you to more people they know. It's a wonderful cycle that starts with your compelling purpose and leads to exceptional client service and a thriving practice.

People do not want to know *what* you do; they want to know *why* you do it.

What Is the Practice You Desire?

In our coaching, we sometimes run across advisors who don't particularly like their practices. They are full of clients who not engaged, who don't value their advice, who are difficult to get in touch with. They do not value what the advisors bring to the relationship. So the practice those advisors desire is just the opposite—a group of people who, over time, they have selected, who do value the advisors, who do respond to requests, and who are engaged to work together in partnership with the advisors to move their financial situations ahead.

Discussion Question

What is the practice you desire? Describe it. How is it the same as, or different from, the practice you were running before you "went through the door" to offering comprehensive financial advice? What are your must-haves in terms of staffing, technology, processes, standards for client interaction, etc.? Write them down.

Decide Who Your Ideal Clients Are

Not everyone is your ideal client. It's important to determine what type of client you want to serve and then focus on that market. We believe people love specialists. If everyone is your client, no one is your client.

We have identified three categories, or types, of clients and have separated them into three different household-income levels. The diagram shows nine different groups of clients. Let's take a look at these groups and discuss whether or not each group is an ideal fit for your practice.

We want you to seek out clients who fall into the bottom four of the six categories in the lower right-hand corner of the table shown on the next page. Your ideal clients (noted in the four spots marked "Yes" in the table) have sufficient income and complex issues, and they are open and receptive to your advice.

Would They Be Ideal Clients for You?

Client Type	Household Income		
	$75,000	$150,000	$300,000+
Self-directed	No	No	No
Opinion-seeking	No	Yes	Yes
Dependent	No	Yes	Yes

1. **Self-directed clients**—These are people who have more time than money. They read financial self-help books, watch investment shows on TV, read financial-advice magazines, invest using online brokerage services, and listen to advice from their neighbors or their barber or hair stylist. They buy the stocks that so-called experts recommend. In essence, they are doing their own brain surgery. They get a little bit of knowledge from various sources and feel equipped to do it all themselves. Worse, they meet with a broker to get good ideas and say, "You know, I think I'm just going to do this myself. I appreciate your advice."

   The reality is, most are weak in implementation, and they typically don't address the complex topics of protection, tax implications, and coordination of legal and tax advisors. They value advice but either get incorrect advice or are reluctant to pay for quality advice. The very worst thing is that many of these people are in our advisors' practices. You may have clients like this. They are a drain on your practice. They want to have you provide them with answers but are not necessarily willing to pay you for your wisdom.

   If a self-directed person had a leaky sink, he would watch a video, go to a home-improvement store to buy some parts, and attempt to fix the leak himself. Professional plumbers love these guys because they make a lot of money cleaning up after them.

   Here is a story that might help you understand how to

communicate effectively with self-directed clients.

One of my coached advisors had a grandfather who was in declining health. He was referred to a land attorney to discuss how to transfer ownership of the grandfather's assets. He called her up and said, "This is my situation, this is who I am, and I have a few questions."

She replied, "I don't do a few questions." (She probably perceived him as a self-directed client.)

He said, "Oh, OK. So how can I work with you?"

"I charge five hundred dollars an hour. I will be glad to meet with you, and I have no doubt I can help your situation." She was only twenty-eight years old yet highly confident about the value she could provide.

When he went to meet with her, he took his checkbook with him. She said, "You will need to pay me in advance for today's meeting." He was a little irritated but wrote her a $500 check and set it on her desk. She didn't touch it.

She asked him to describe the situation. He went through it. She drew a couple of pictures and asked him a dozen questions. Then she said, "Here is how we can structure this." She described a strategy, then said, "It will take two more meetings, and you will have what you need."

When the grandfather died, he owned nothing, which is exactly what he had wanted. He did not own a car or his farm anymore; all he owned was his clothes. It was all given away the way he wanted it done, and his survivors saved hundreds of thousands of dollars on estate taxes. All for only $1,500.

The attorney knew her value, and she was not going to let the client self-direct her. She was not going to let him pick her brain and then walk out of there without paying her anything. It might be difficult to do this at first, but it gets easier, especially if you are convinced of the value you provide.

2. **Opinion-seeking clients**—These are typically busy, successful people who have more money than time. They are too busy to do financial planning themselves. They invest in the best efforts of others. They know they need advice. They recognize they need someone to help them with implementation, discipline, and follow-through. They are succeeding in their careers and want to work with advisors who are succeeding in *their* careers.

3. **Dependent clients**—For clients in this category, money is a foreign language. They are somewhat intimidated by money. They could be working in valuable occupations—as veterinarians or teachers, for example—but their work is not related to business. They tend to hand the reins over to somebody else. Unfortunately, they are quite vulnerable to bad advice. They want and value advice and know they cannot handle their own financial planning, nor do they want to do it themselves. They are not self-directed. They say, "I need help, but I don't know even what questions to ask."

Now let's look at each type of client in each income category. The guidelines we are about to share are extremely accurate.

A self-directed client with a household income of about $50,000 is not the ideal client for our advisors. He or she might be a good client for another company that markets to that segment of the population. Yes, that person needs help, but serving him or her from the practice you're building is similar to a patient going to a brain surgeon for a cold.

Self-directed clients in the $150,000 and $300,000 income categories are not ideal clients for our advisors, either. Why? Because they want to do it all themselves. They are not likely to engage in an ongoing financial advice relationship with an advisor. It is fatiguing trying to get clients like this to provide documents, agree to a financial strategy, and follow recommendations.

It is possible that some opinion-seeking clients who have about

$50,000 in household income might be good prospects for our advisors because they value our services and expertise, especially if they are vertically mobile in their careers. You have to be careful with this category, though, because our services might be expensive for them. In many cases, they have high demands and expectations, but they are never going to make a lot of household income. There are probably better companies for them to work with.

Opinion-seeking clients who earn between $150,000 and $300,000 or above in annual household income typically make fantastic clients for us. These are the people with sufficient household income, their issues are typically complex, they are busy people, and they don't have time to do their own financial planning. They need help. They need knowledge and discipline, and they are great candidates for financial advice. They will fit into your practice very well.

Dependent clients who are making about $50,000 a year need help, and many of our advisors may point them toward resources just because they want to. But you have to be careful that you don't end up balancing their checkbook for them. We often refer them to a bank to establish a relationship, and sometimes that is all they need.

Dependent clients who earn $150,000 to $300,000 and above make fantastic clients because they tend to value advice and benefit from it.

 **Discussion Question**

Who are your ideal clients? Describe them as specifically as possible, in terms of demographics, life stage, profession, attitude/mindset, etc. Write down these criteria, and then determine which of your current clients match this profile and which ones do not.

Fire Clients Appropriately when It's Necessary

While we are on the topic of acquiring clients, it might be helpful to discuss the opposite—how to quit working with clients who are annoying or abusive or just don't fit into the demographic you want to focus on. We have known of clients who were actually destructive to an advisor's practice. We hear of this happening more often than you might expect. Clients will ask for a lot more service than they want to pay for, or they treat an advisor or team member, or their time, with disrespect.

We have an advisor in Iowa named Bill. He had a client who was extremely demanding and rude to Bill's team members. Bill asked the client to behave more professionally, but he did not. Eventually Bill got up the courage to let the client know he could not work with him anymore. Then we found out that Bill got the client as a recommendation from another advisor who had gotten tired of working with him.

If you have a prospect you do not wish to work with, for whatever reason, a tactful way to handle that is simply to say, "My practice is not taking new clients right now." Exiting a relationship with an established client might take a little more courage. You are not obligated to give a specific reason. You could say something like, "I am narrowing the focus of my practice and have decided to serve only (fill in the blank—e.g., "those in the medical profession" or "high-net-worth individuals").

 **Discussion Question**

Have you ever fired a client? What was your reason? Looking back on it now, do you believe it was the right decision? Are there any clients you need to fire now?

Be Clear About What You Charge

Vanguard® released a study in 2020 titled "The Value of Advice: Assessing the Role of Emotions." The study found that most advised investors are not knowledgeable about what financial advice costs. While most of the respondents knew *how* they were paying for advice, less than half knew *how much* they paid.[34]

A co-author of the paper stressed the great opportunity this presents for advisors.

"This lack of investor comprehension in regards to how much they pay for advice highlights an opportunity for the industry to disclose fees in a more clear and transparent manner," Cynthia Pagliaro, a senior researcher in the Vanguard Investment Strategy Group, wrote. "Cost transparency would greatly benefit advisors, as it would enable them to better articulate the value of their service to clients in relation to the fees they charge."

Prune Your Client List

Todd Bramson, one of North Star's top advisors whom we mentioned in chapter 2, began to prune his client list a while back so he could focus more of his time and attention on his best clients.

He said, "I don't want to work with people who present me with an unsolvable problem, such as, 'I'm close to retirement, but I haven't saved enough, and I don't want to save enough. Help me retire successfully.' That is not an ideal client."

Todd defined three main goals for the way he wants his practice to run—he wants to work less, grow his practice, and have more fun. Those are his three themes.

On the surface, it seems like it would be difficult to accomplish three of those goals at the same time. To accomplish that, he sat down and decided which clients to focus his time and effort on and

---

34. "Vanguard® Measures the Emotional Value of Financial Advice," Vanguard press release, April 1, 2020, https://pressroom.vanguard.com/news/Press-Release-Vanguard-Measures-Emotional-Value-of-Advice-04012020.html.

which clients to invite to find other advisors. Here are just some of the strategies Todd used to move toward his new three-tiered statement of purpose:

1. Simplify, and say *no*!
2. Be honest and polite (but direct).
3. Make health my number one priority. (Be happier and healthier: "vacation Todd").
4. Work only with top-tier clients (AAA and AA).
5. Avoid rushing; leave a margin for error.
6. Allow no drama or stress; don't overreact to people and issues (especially the market and things I cannot control).

Most advisors find that their focus and their priorities change as they evolve in their careers. New advisors focus on establishing client relationships and building their practices. But in later years, once their clientele is established, they can make room for new goals.

Segment Your Clients

Now, even if you seek out the ideal clients we just described, you will still end up with your best clients, your average clients, and your least-enjoyable clients. You want to treat your best clients with the highest possible level of service. To do that, we recommend segmenting your clientele. This is a good strategy in any sales-or service-related profession.

To demonstrate the concept of segmenting clients, let's use another example about automobiles.

Let's say you have a high-end car—maybe a Lexus. The people who typically drive Lexus models have higher-than-average income.

If you go to a Lexus dealership for servicing, you will probably get great service—coffee, music, and they might loan you a car you can use while they are working on yours. It's a clean, quiet, and pleasant environment. There's no grease or noise. They might have quiet computer nooks where you can do some work. Overall, every aspect of your visit to the Lexus dealership is extremely pleasant.

Now, there are a lot of good cars on the market that are more affordable than a Lexus, but most of them are not at the same level in terms of quality, features, or performance. They cost less, and it costs less to service them. They are manufactured for the middle class. Volkswagen is one example. I've had Volkswagens and found them to be reliable. But they're not in the Lexus tier.

Let's say you now take your daughter's car to a Volkswagen dealership for service. You aren't likely to get the white-glove service you got from Lexus. It will be more like a transaction. The waiting area might not be as plush, quiet, and clean. But you are still a valued client.

In essence, that is segmentation.

The diagram shown next identifies criteria you could use to segment your clients.

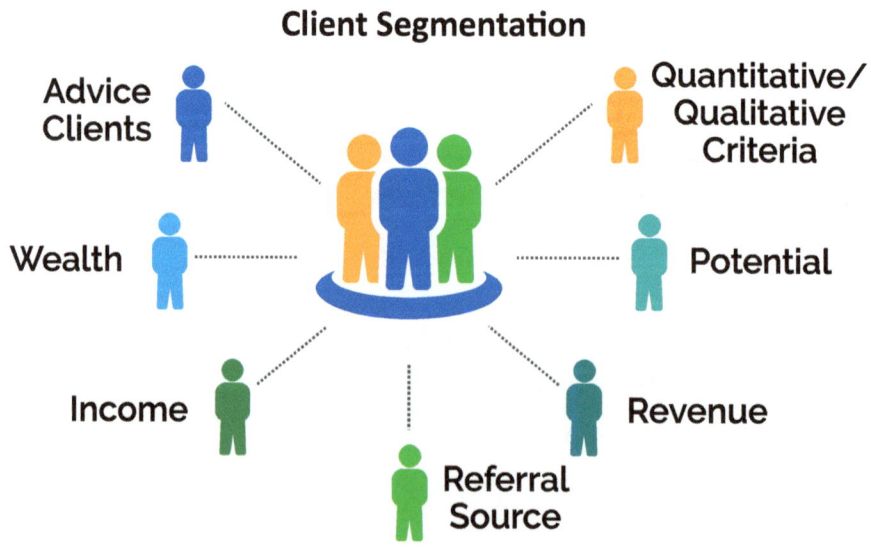

Client Segmentation

Advice Clients

Quantitative/ Qualitative Criteria

Wealth

Potential

Income

Revenue

Referral Source

Discussion Question

Have you ever segmented your clients? If not, make that an action item. Determine which clients fit into which categories. Then prune your client list so you can devote more of your time and energy to your best clients.

To Create a Practice Full of Ideal Clients, Build Your Prospect List

Once you determine who your ideal clients are and segment your client list, we recommend making a list of prospects among your current clients whom you want to approach about your ongoing-advice practice. Knowing the type of practice you want and the types of clients you want to serve makes it easier to build your ideal clientele.

Then you can focus on anticipating and preparing for your client meetings to introduce what's in this relationship for them. Use the scripts we provide in chapter 5. Expand the breadth and meaning of your advice. Practice at the top of your license.

It's a lot more rewarding to run a Practice on Purpose and to have a clear vision of why you are here. Your ongoing-advice practice will enable you to achieve your vision, values, and purpose, and your clients will find value from your work and in their own goal achievement. As a result, you will achieve the financial services practice you desire and your clients deserve.

Client of the Advisor or Client of the Practice?

This is a subtle distinction yet can make a real difference. Early in a career, it's natural for advisors to think of clients as *their* clients. Yet once they have built a client base of a hundred or more clients, this can be problematic. The clients are accustomed to being serviced and contacted by the advisor personally. Unless the advisor can redefine this relationship, they may get boxed in and unable to grow.

If the clients know they are clients of the *practice* rather than an *advisor*, the advisor can have his or her staff and other advisors on the team be contact points. This expands the practice capacity and makes it easier to segment clients and have the right people provide the appropriate service to the clients.

So, right from the start, we recommend using the phrase, "You are a client of the practice, and we look forward to working together for many years." Often on the advisor's website, we will picture the team members, even if they are specialists at North Star. When the advisor eventually gets his or her own team members, we add them as well. We have found that clients want to be clients of a practice more than clients of an individual. It enlarges the relationship from both perspectives.

What Tears Apart a Practice

Now, let's see how this concept plays out in a financial advisor's practice. Let's say one of your average clients starts calling you a lot and wanting to meet with you. He has a lot of questions. You accommodate him, but you realize you're spending a lot more time with him than you are with some of your more valuable clients.

Pretty soon, this client is elevating himself to the level of Lexus service. If you're not aware what he means in your practice, yet you give him Lexus service, he is getting a heck of a deal—you are not. When this happens, it means the client is choosing the service model—you are not.

Then your best, most valuable clients might not be getting the time and attention they deserve from you because you're spending it all on your average clients—your "Volkswagen clients." We have watched this happen in practices, and it turns them upside down. This is what tears a practice apart.

Once you transform your practice to an advice-based model, those clients who are paying you for advice—the Lexus clients—must receive the white-glove service—the Lexus service.

The diagram below illustrates this concept. Volkswagen clients are demanding Lexus service. They are elevating themselves to get an amount of attention that is not appropriate for the amount they're paying. Because the advisor does not realize they are Volkswagen clients, they take advantage of the advisor's expertise without paying what it's worth. By default, then the Lexus clients do not receive the time they deserve. Or worse, the Lexus clients are getting the same level of service as the Volkswagen clients, yet paying more for the same service.

To avoid this scenario, advisors need to know who the Volkswagen clients are and who the Lexus clients are and give them the level of service that's commensurate with their contribution to practice revenue.

Again, the advisor needs to run the client service model—not the clients.

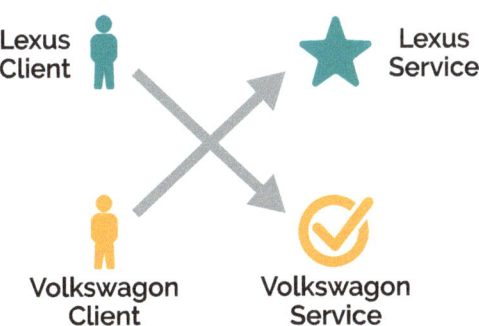

Now, your best and most valuable clients aren't necessarily those who bring in the most revenue each year. Maybe they bring you a lot of referrals. Maybe they are advocates for you and your practice. Maybe they have a lot of potential for becoming clients who do bring in more revenue at some point.

You can look at quantitative or qualitative criteria, yet you need some sort of specific criteria to determine in which segments your clients belong.

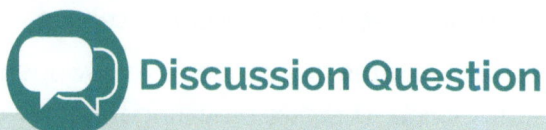

Discussion Question

What are the segments you have defined for your client list? Do you have AAA, AA, and A clients? Do you have Platinum, Gold, and Silver clients? Or Tier 1, Tier 2, and Tier 3? What type of hierarchy will be easy for you and your staff to follow, to remind you of the importance of giving your best service to your best clients?

Follow the Pareto Principle, or 80/20 Rule

The Pareto Principle, named after highly respected economist Vilfredo Pareto (1848–1923) , specifies that 80 percent of consequences come from 20 percent of the causes. This principle, also known as "the 80/20 rule," reminds us there typically isn't an equal balance between inputs and outputs.

In terms of your practice, you will discover, at some point, that about 20 percent of your clients drive about 80 percent of your revenue. Or it might be a 30/70 split. But it's somewhere in that neighborhood.

It's important to know which of your clients are among the 20 percent who account for most of the revenue in your practice. Simply determine your criteria for segmentation and then place each of your clients in one of those three categories. Once you do that, then you will create a menu of services that contains three different levels of service, appropriate for your three levels of clients.

Discussion Question

Pareto is alive and well—20 percent of your clients drive 80 percent of your revenue. Which of your current clients are among your top 20 percent? Why? What will you do to attract more clients who have similar characteristics?

Develop and Use a Three-Tiered Menu of Services

The menu of services is a description of what each segment will receive from your practice, you, your team, and your associates. It can include aspects of service such as the frequency of meetings, the scope of engagement, response time, invitations to seminars and events, access to technology, and types of reports you generate for them.

The diagram shown next is an example of a menu of services, with three levels described: holistic wealth management, investment advisory (with a portfolio minimum), and transactional.

Sample Menu

How we help clients

	Financial topics	Financial plan	Meetings/Contacts	Pricing model
Holistic wealth management[1]	**Integrated analysis on the following areas:** Investment planning, Protection planning[1], Current financial position, Retirement planning, FINANCIAL PLANNING, Tax planning, Estate planning[1]	**Yes** Customized written recommendations provided to help you achieve your unique financial goals	• Comprehensive annual analysis based on life/financial events • Semi-annual review of progress made • Active approach to plan implementation strategies and follow up[1] • Ongoing goal tracking	Annual fee for financial plan varies based on complexity
Investment advisory (Portfolio minimum)	• Diverse asset allocation • Portfolio rebalancing as necessary • Tax advantaged strategies	No	• Annual review to align account portfolio with client goals, time horizon and investment objective • Review as requested	Asset management fee based on account type and size
Transactional[2]	• Products provided based on client's desire or gap analysis	No	Contact related to product/account service	Commission earned on product/investments provided

Insurance and investment products will have product-level expenses

*Financial Professionals do not provide tax or legal advice. Please consult a tax or legal professional for advice regarding your specific situation.

1 Separate from the financial plan and our role as financial planner, we may recommend the purchase of specific investment or insurance products or accounts. These product recommendations are not part of the financial plan and you are under no obligation to follow them.

2 These activities are not investment advisory services.

The lowest tier of clients[35]—Volkswagen clients, if you will—are mostly transactional clients. Maybe they bought a disability income policy, a long-term care insurance policy, or an annuity from you. It was a single-need product sale. These are quite common, especially for advisors who are in the early years of their careers.

The middle level is typically investment advisory (IA) clients. Those are the people whose assets you are managing and investing.

It can be difficult to quantify the clients in this category. Do you include everyone whose clients you are managing, or just those whose assets are at a certain threshold? When will they need the money? Will it be qualified or non-qualified?

Some people say this middle level of service is a lazy pricing model. You get a percentage of AUM, but that's it. You engage with

---

35. Clients within particular tiers may typically select a category of services (transactional, investment advisory, or financial planning). However, their tier does not determine the services they receive. The relationship between client tier and services provided is a generalized representation of our client base.

those clients frequently because of compliance and because of their expectations.

The top tier—the Lexus tier of service—typically receives comprehensive financial advice, which some refer to as "holistic wealth management." These are the areas of financial planning designations such as the CFP® or ChFC® cover. This list of services is comprehensive. It includes a financial plan, meetings throughout the year, and an ongoing partnership with you to establish their financial plans and adjust them over time, as their life situations change.

Here is a summary of the three tiers:

Segment/Tier	Typical Service
Top tier	Comprehensive financial advice
Middle tier	Investment advisory (IA)
Third tier	Protection and transactions

Here is that same concept, simplified:

Segment/Tier	Typical Service
Top segment	Exceptional service
Middle segment	Good service
Third segment	OK service

Have Your Clients Choose Their Level of Engagement

It could be difficult, or at least awkward, to tell your clients you are assigning them to the second or third tier. A better strategy is to have your clients choose their own level of engagement. Show them the menu of services, describe each of the three tiers, answer their questions, and they will decide on their own what they need and can afford.

Simply ask them, "Now that you're seen and heard about the three levels of engagement in our practice, how do you want to work together?"

You can certainly steer them toward or away from a category.

Once you've done this with all your clients, now your segmentation is complete. Now you can more accurately provide the level of service that is appropriate for the level of engagement.

Know Your Clients: The MacKay 66

When I was in college, I worked at a gas station. One day, a businessman pulled up in his car and asked me, "Hey, could you drive me back to my company, bring my car back here, and change my oil?"

I said, "OK, sure." I did what he asked, and it became a regular thing. He would show up about every six weeks, and I would drop him off at this company called MacKay Envelope.

When he first introduced himself to me, he said, "I'm Harvey MacKay."

I said, "I'm Gary Schwartz."

He asked me if I was going to school, and I said yes, I was a student at the University of Minnesota.

He replied, "I'm the CEO of MacKay Envelope. I'm also on the board of trustees for the University of Minnesota."

I said, "Mr. MacKay, pleasure to meet you."

He became a columnist for the local newspaper. (Today, he writes a weekly column that offers career and inspirational advice, and it is featured in more than one hundred newspapers.)

He used to write about "The MacKay 66." It was a list of the sixty-six things any person in sales should know about a client. I still have that list. The idea is that the more you know about your clients, the easier it is to create deep, meaningful relationships with them. The list includes details like where your clients went to college, what was the best book they've ever read, and where they last went on vacation.

When I graduated from college, Mr. MacKay handed me my diploma. And then, maybe twenty-five years later, when he retired, I hired his assistant to be my assistant. She worked with me for almost ten years. MacKay is the author of seven *New York Times* bestselling books, including three number-one bestsellers. One title you might recognize is *Swim with the Sharks Without Being Eaten Alive: Outsell, Outmanage, Outmotivate, and Outnegotiate Your Competition*.

The point is, know your clients well—not just the surface facts that other people know, but what makes them tick, what they love, what has shaped them to be the people they are.

 **Discussion Question**

How well do you know your clients, beyond the surface demographic details? What will you do to get to know them better? How could your practice benefit by cultivating deeper relationships with your clients?

How This Comes Together

Before we move to chapter 4, let's review important strategies for building the type of practice you desire. They are all key elements in how the wonderful world of comprehensive financial advice works:

- Identify and articulate your why—your purpose. Why are you an advisor?

- Lead with advice, not solutions.

- Move beyond competition to an intimate connection with your clients.

- Decide who your ideal clients are.

- Segment your clients.

- Use a menu of services.

- Lead your clients to achieve health, wealth, and happiness—while also achieving the same for yourself.

- Now you are offering the right advice to the right clients!

With these strategies, you will achieve the practice you desire. Now let's explore achieving the practice your clients deserve.

CHAPTER 4

ACHIEVING THE PRACTICE YOUR CLIENTS DESERVE

A key part of building the financial practice *you desire* is creating the practice *your clients deserve*. Both sides of the equation are equally important.

In chapter 3, we discussed how to build a practice you desire. Now let's discuss the practice your clients deserve. We'll start by describing six valuable benefits your clients receive in an ongoing advice relationship.

Six Valuable Benefits Your Clients Receive in an Ongoing Advice Relationship

Clients might ask you, "You're going to charge me a fee for financial advice. What exactly do I get for that fee?" Even if they don't ask the question, they are thinking about it. Our good friend, Mitch Anthony, lists the following six valuable benefits when we provide them with advice:

1. **Organization**—We help bring order to people's financial lives. We organize their shoeboxes full of receipts and financial statements.

2. **Accountability**—We will help them follow through on their financial commitments.

3. **Objectivity**—We bring insight from the outside to help them avoid emotionally driven decisions in important money matters.

4. **Proactivity**—We work with them to anticipate their life transitions and to be financially prepared for them. Time spent in preparation avoids time spent in reparation.

5. **Education**—We explore and provide the specific knowledge they need to help them succeed in their situations. We share our knowledge, experience, and expertise with them.

6. **Partnership**—We work in concert with each client and other advisors, such as accountants and attorneys, to make his or her plan come alive.

Notice these six benefits don't describe any products; instead, they describe the value you bring to your clients from engaging in an ongoing advice relationship.

 **Discussion Question**

In addition to the six benefits and areas of value listed above, what other specific types of benefits do your clients receive from your ongoing advice?

50 Things You Do for Your Clients

In 2016, Putnam Investments released a one-page document titled "50 Things: What a Professional Financial Advisor Does for You." It was directed toward prospects and clients, to demonstrate the unparalleled value they receive from working with a financial advisor.

Here is just a small sample of the benefits on that list:[36]

---

36. "50 Things: What a Professional Financial Advisor Does for You," William Smith, Putnam Investments, reprinted from Horsesmouth LLC, 2016.

A professional advisor:

1. Cares more about you and your money than anyone who doesn't share your last name (financial planning).

2. Formalizes your goals and puts them in writing (financial planning).

3. Prepares an asset allocation for you so you can achieve the best rate of return for a given level of risk tolerance (investments).

4. Suggests alternatives to increase your income during retirement (investments).

5. Repositions investments to take full advantage of tax law provisions (taxes).

6. Works with your tax and legal advisors to guide you in meeting your financial goals (taxes).

7. Monitors changes in your life and family situation (person-to-person).

8. Shares the experience of dozens or hundreds of clients who have faced circumstances similar to yours.

Leading Clients to a Better Place

This is our favorite definition of leadership—it applies to advisors leading clients, just as it pertains to those of us who lead advisors:

> Leadership is about taking someone to a place they would not have gone on their own that is better for them.

The concept originates from the great German philosopher Johann Wolfgang von Goethe. He said, "If I accept you as you are, I will make you worse; however, if I treat you as though you are what you are capable of becoming, I help you become that."

This is the essence of what you, as a skilled advisor, can do for your clients through your advice, wisdom, discipline, and compassion. We all need leadership because, as humans, we are incapable of seeing ourselves as the world sees us. It's our blind spot. We need leadership to become our full selves.

As an advisor, you can complete that picture for your clients by guiding them in realizing their hopes, fears, desires, and knowledge about their own finances. We cannot do our own brain surgery or even cut our own hair. There are just some things we cannot do effectively on our own. Managing our financial resources in an expert way is one of those things. We are our own worst enemies.

People who do better financially likely have an advisor, and those advisors are probably worth every penny for the change they make. Leadership in our society is too rare, and we know it when we see it. It changes everything. Wise clients seek out advisors who can serve them in this leadership role.

As advisors, we need to value and deliver on our leadership skills. We are taking our clients—and frankly, ourselves—to a place we would not have gone on our own, and we are all better for it.

 **Discussion Question**

Think about what it means to "take someone to a place they would not have gone on their own that is better for them." What does this mean to you as an advice-based advisor? Write down three to five *specific* ways in which you will provide this type of priceless leadership to your clients.

Practice at the Top of Your License

We are all licensed. We can do basic commodity sales, which are transactions. They are sales. That is the lower part of the license—the table stakes just to be in our profession.

But to help people live richly—not die rich—we can practice at the *top* of our license. It's the highest-functioning thing you can do with the abilities, privileges, and permission you have while working with your clients.

People are not paying you just to build a plan; they are also paying you to *adjust* that plan over time, as their needs and the environment change. That's top-level thinking. A doctor can help you get healthier temporarily by alleviating a pain or stitching up a wound, but the really good doctors help you get—and stay—healthier over time.

To practice at the top of your license is to use your unique talents, knowledge, and compassion to make it possible for your clients to live that best life possible.

George Bernard Shaw said, "Most people die with their music inside of them." We believe this. Be purposeful about using all your potential to optimize the value you provide to your clients.

 **Discussion Question**

What does "practicing at the top of your license" mean to you? What differentiates you from other advisors who have the same licenses?

Creating an Advice-Based Practice Often Requires a Change in Mindset

An advice-based practice is one in which your clients pay you a financial planning or a financial advice fee year after year. It's *ongoing financial advice*.

Here is an important note of clarification. A small subset of advisors out there provides *advice only*. They do not engage in product sales of any kind. They charge only for their advice and require their clients to get their product solutions somewhere else. That is not the model we advocate. We believe in building an advice-based practice—one that blends expert advice with the appropriate financial solutions.

Also, some advisors let their IA underwrite their financial advice. This means they are giving clients their advice for free. Is this a sound business model in the long term? We believe it is important to recognize these are two distinctly different services.

The first step in creating a truly advice-based practice is to change your mindset. Providing financial advice for a fee means that you, the advisor, are the product. It's personal. This goes back to the fact that you have the mind of a capitalist and the heart of a social worker.

Your clients are benefiting from you personally—you as a unique and quality human being, as well as your knowledge as a professional, your compassion, and your hopes and dreams for them. Financial planning software is useful, yet you and your advice are the true catalysts.

Financial Advice Has Its Own Value

In the traditional financial advice practice, we viewed our value to clients as a wide array of options in terms of financial products and services. But moving to a financial-advice practice requires that we see financial advice as having its own value. Our financial advice is the offering.

The old model was that agents represented *their companies*, or carriers, to prospects. With financial advice, we represent *our clients* and go find solutions for their needs. That is a key differentiator. We do not start with a solution.

Your Clients Need Your Wisdom

There is a huge difference between advice and information. People are drowning in data and information, and they are starved for knowledge and wisdom.

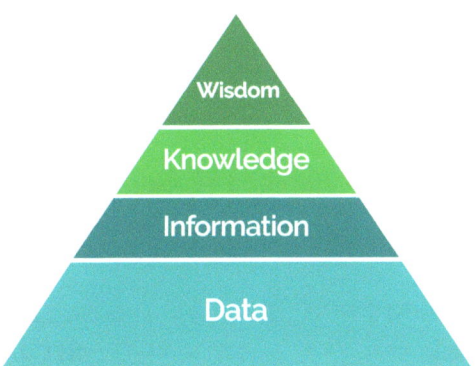

People can spend all day on the internet, evaluating data, news reports, and journal articles. What your clients are paying for is your unique blend of knowledge, wisdom, experience, and commitment to guiding their financial path. This cumulative value is based on their situation, what you know about their situation, and the experience and insight you have gained by engaging in many other client meetings over the years.

When you go to a surgeon, you are not paying him or her just for the surgery you will undergo; you are really buying the two thousand other surgeries like yours the surgeon has already performed. Similarly, if you are an advisor with a large client base, your clients are buying your experience in providing advice to those two or three hundred other clients.

Ed likes to tell the story about a woman who has a squeaky wood floor in her house. She hires a local carpenter to come fix the squeak. The gentleman walks in the house, enters the room with the squeaky floor, takes a few steps, and locates the source of the squeak near a corner. He pulls out a nail and pounds it into the floor. The squeak is gone. The woman is very grateful and asks him, "How much do I owe you?"

He says, "You owe me one hundred dollars."

Her jaw drops. "One hundred dollars! You were here for only two minutes. Can you give me an itemized receipt on the hundred dollars?"

"No problem." He pulls out a piece of paper, and here's what he writes:

Itemized Receipt

The nail	$ 1.00
Knowing where to put the nail	99.00
Total	**$100.00**

Just like that carpenter, your lifetime of cumulative experience represents knowledge and wisdom to your clients. Those who engage in a financial-advice relationship with you can tap into that wealth of knowledge and wisdom at any time.

The need for financial advice has never, ever been greater. Now, more than ever, people are dependent on someone to help them make good financial decisions. Increasingly, they must depend on their own resources and not on government resources. That means there is more opportunity than ever for you to make a positive impact in people's lives.

A study released in April 2021 revealed Americans' high levels of financial anxiety, even before the pandemic. The study says 60 percent of respondents indicated feeling anxious when *thinking* about their personal finances, while 50 percent indicated feeling stressed when *discussing* their finances. Also, 65 percent of women indicated feeling anxious about their personal finances, compared to 54 percent of men. Major factors contributing to high levels of financial anxiety and stress include a lack of assets and insufficient income, high debt, money-management challenges and low financial literacy. Even prior to the pandemic, more than half of American adults were experiencing financial anxiety.[37]

People need ongoing advice relationships with advisors. Their ability to save for retirement depends on your knowledge, wisdom, and expertise. Advice is knowledge in action.

Guide Your Clients Past the Trilogy of Obstacles

As you know all too well, three of the biggest obstacles that prevent many people from taking charge of their finances are denial, procrastination, and pride. By understanding how these mindsets stand in people's way to financial confidence, you can educate them patiently while offering them empathy and compassion.

Let's look at these three roadblocks in more detail.

1. Denial

Denial is one of the biggest obstacles that prevents people from taking charge of their financial well-being.

People don't wake up naturally thinking that they're going to seek you out to take care of important financial-planning matters. No, they wake up in the morning thinking they have plenty of time. Death is something that happens a long way down the road. As a result, they have no sense of urgency about getting their finances in order.

Your wise advice provides your clients with a virtual shield that

_____

37. "Large Number of Americans Reported Financial Anxiety and Stress Even Before the Pandemic," FINRA press release, April 28, 2021, https://www.finra.org/media-center/newsreleases/2021/large-number-americans-reported-financial-anxiety-and-stress-even.

protects them and their families from the negative consequences of failing to plan early.

We have to initiate those tough conversations. That's not always easy, but it's necessary.

2. Procrastination

Procrastination is the second big obstacle people face when it comes to managing their finances. We've all struggled with procrastination. We know we need to do something important, but we put it off—until tomorrow. Or later.

Too often, people don't get serious about financial matters until they become emergencies. When do people get serious about retirement? A few years before they retire. When do they get serious about saving for their child's education? That happens, typically, when their child is only a year or two away from college. Now, all of a sudden, they want to start saving for college, and they realize they would be much farther along if they had started much sooner.

And when do they get serious about having the right insurance protection? Unfortunately, many times that happens when they get a worrisome diagnosis from their doctor. Now, suddenly, their mortality becomes a reality.

But unfortunately, when those trigger moments occur for your clients, it's too late. We have to instill in them that sense of urgency.

Most people have good intentions, but intentions mean nothing until they become actions, through implementation. The biggest gap is the one between intentions and implementation. It is our job to close that gap. We have to inspire our clients to take action. The inspiration leads to the implementation—and then the implementation *becomes* the inspiration.

Clients feel great about following your wise advice, and they begin making changes in their lives. Even if those changes are small, they add up. Before long, your clients begin to see and experience the difference your advice is making in their lives.

Maybe they are worrying less about money. Maybe they are making progress toward an important financial goal. Maybe they feel more in control and more knowledgeable about where they stand.

As your clients' advisor, you are the catalyst for them to take action toward securing their financial future.

3. Pride

Pride is another obstacle that prevents many people from taking charge of their finances. Many people don't want to look foolish to others. Let's face it—we've all made some poor financial choices in our lifetime—for example, failing to save, being underinsured, or maybe having bad credit.

The longer people put those important actions off, the more embarrassed they are. No one wants to divulge or confess their shortcomings to financial advisors—or anyone else.

 **Discussion Question**

Of the three obstacles listed here—denial, procrastination, and pride—which one have you observed among clients most often? What have you done to guide your clients past such obstacles? To what extent can you do an even better job of minimizing the impact of those obstacles on your clients' behavior and forward progress?

Use Your Four Unique Gifts

At North Star Resource Group, we require all new financial advisors to take our Advisor Oath. On the first day of orientation with the new group of people, we stress to them the importance of understanding what their job is and what their gifts to the world are. You certainly bring many additional valuable attributes to your client relationships, but in our Advisor's Oath, we address four important gifts: finding, educating, inspiring, and motivating clients.

Here is the oath:

Advisor's Oath

I hereby solemnly swear from this day forward, it is my obligation and responsibility to help my clients start and stay the course to financial security, and that begins by finding, educating, motivating, and inspiring people to take action on their financial future so that they can start and stay the course to financial security.

Let's look at these four important gifts.

1. Finding Clients

Finding is a gentler way to say "prospecting."

Earlier, we cited research studies that point to the vast need for your advice in this country. Finding clients today isn't difficult at all.

Once you find them, you become their intervention specialist. It starts with going out and initiating those important conversations with clients, knowing that they are facing various obstacles to becoming your client.

2. Educating Clients

Great advisors understand that they are great educators. In an advice-based practice, you are doing more educating than selling. When you educate your clients, they will understand and acknowledge your value; you won't have to *convince* them of it.

3. Motivating Clients

Once your clients understand the great value in having you partner with them to prepare for whatever lies ahead, they will be relieved they found you. They will be motivated take the necessary actions in following your advice.

4. Inspiring Clients

Once your clients begin to see results from implementing your advice, your continued guidance will inspire them to keep going. They will be "all in" when it comes to working with you to monitor their financial situations and make adjustments as needed.

Make it your mission to inspire people to start and stay the course to financial confidence. When you do that, you will see them make tremendous strides in their financial well-being.

Language Is Everything when You Are the Product

Once you recognize that you are the product, it's then important to understand how the language you use when speaking with clients can elevate the advice you provide.

I have a stack of note cards next to my desk. When I hear a great phrase, I write it down on a card and add it to my stack. I've been doing that since 1977, and now I have around five hundred cards. I study these cards to improve and practice my language. I'll choose a phrase in the morning and then try to incorporate it into what I say that day. It's really helpful.

Without an advisor, most people will earn a fortune in their lifetime, yet they may not have much to show for it.

The right advice at the right time can make all the difference. Choose your language carefully. Language is a powerful tool we have as leaders and as advisors. The more intentional we are with our language, the more we can influence our clients to follow our advice. The language you use creates the picture clients have in their minds of what you are offering.

While conducting a workshop with advisors recently, a top performer said he has been asking his clients this important question: "What is the one thing you would regret most in your life if you don't do it?"

One of his clients, a surgeon specializing in facial reconstruction, replied, "I've always wanted to volunteer for a year with Doctors Without Borders. That's something I will regret—if I don't take a year off and go to a disadvantaged country to apply my skills."

Once the advisor reviewed the surgeon's financial plan, he saw that this was doable. He told him, "If your hospital permits it, you can do this."

By selecting his language carefully, this advisor added considerable value to his client—not just as a financial advisor, but also as a life coach.

We recommend asking yourself this question, too. As you build your career and legacy, what is the one thing *you* will regret if you don't do it?

One of our top advisors at North Star refers to himself as a "professional visitor."

He visits with people, just like all advisors do, but he has a unique ability to create powerful images in his clients' minds and hearts simply by the language he uses when he speaks with them. That is one trait that makes his clients value him so much.

Most people are pretty casual about their language; they don't think much about what they are going to say. They just ramble their way through client meetings. What a waste of potential!

> "The limits of my language mean the limits of my world."

Ludwig Wittgenstein

There are people who build entire careers around the powerful potential of language to persuade people and to influence the way they think and act. It's about pausing at the right time and for the right amount of time; asking open-ended, thoughtful questions; listening intently and repeating clients' concerns to them; and planning in advance what questions or phrases a particular client wants and needs to hear from you.

Language varies a lot by culture. In America, when we meet someone, we tend to ask, "What do you do?" In Asia, people are more likely to ask, "How is your family?" or they will say, "Tell me about your family." If you are in Scandinavia, apparently they ask, "What are your hobbies?"

Language is one of the powerful tools we have, as advisors, that differentiates us. When the words change, the conversations changes. And until the words change, the conversation will not change.

Try Using These Phrases

In your client meetings, try to phrase your recommendations in a way that reminds them that you are partnering with them to help them get what they want. Be intentional about your language; choose your words and phrases carefully. Clients are meeting with you for what is in it for them. They do it for their reasons, not yours. They want to know what the expected outcome of an action is. They don't want a sales pitch.

That is why a phrase like "We want to work with you on building a confident retirement" is preferable to saying, "You need an annuity." Focus the discussion on what *they* can accomplish by working with you. Maybe they want to send their children to any college that will take them or to buy a vacation home overseas.

Here are some other terms we prefer:

Instead of This:	Try Saying This:
Agency	Firm
Agent	Financial professional
Employee	Team member
Selling	Advising, consulting, recommending
Recruiting	Selecting
Referrals	Recommendations
Cost	Investment
Industry	Profession

Regarding the last entry in the table above, using the word "profession" instead of "industry" has become more important to us as we evolve further into advice-based practices.

"Industry" denotes that something is manufactured and then distributed, and that may have been the case when insurance companies had agents and operated with more of a manufacturing distribution model. Today, we represent our clients to the manufacturers. We represent the clients to solutions. We are advocates for our clients, which means we are in a profession. We are professionals helping clients achieve financial security and financial success. We believe that, by referring to ourselves as being part of a *profession* rather than an *industry*, we will elevate the way we think about ourselves and how clients view us as well.

Now, here are some more suggestions about language. Two of our favorite conversation-starting phrases for advisors to use in client meetings are "I've noticed that..." and "If I could show you a way..."

Here are four phrases to use to move your conversation along in a way that makes sense for the client:

1. **"Money is a wonderful servant and a terrible master."** You can build a conversation around this topic with your clients. It will allow you to discuss with them how stressful it can be if money is their master. It's a concept that most people relate to and can grasp quickly.

2. **"We want to make that money work harder for you than you are working for the money. If I can show you a way to make that happen, would you be interested?"** When you use that language with your client, it means you might invest her money in American corporations that are deriving value for profit, and the client will benefit from that value through her investments. So while she is working hard, you are going to get her money to work hard, too. People like the notion of getting their money to work for them versus thinking it is sitting in a dormant account.

3. **"Most people will earn a fortune in their lifetime. Without an advisor, they may not have much to show for it."** When many people look at their tax returns, they say, "Wow, where did the money go?" People who have an advisor typically know where the money went, and they still have some of it left. We all face the lure of relentless consumerism. Our society encourages us to purchase things all the time. If you are not disciplined about your money, you will succumb to that temptation to indulge—"I want it now, I want to have fun, and I want to live." People do some incredible rationalizing about frittering away their money. John Schubert, an advisor at Ameriprise and a well-known speaker, often says that advisors keep people from "spending money they don't have on things they don't need to impress people they don't like."

4. **"The right advice at the right time can make all the difference."** As advisors, we manage emotions more than we manage money. If you stay in close contact with your clients, you will know when they are facing major life changes that can cause them to experience a lot of emotions—either positive or negative—around their money. Being there to guide them during such challenging times can make a huge difference, both in earning clients' trust and in helping them make wise decisions when they might not be thinking clearly.

These are important phrases because they lead your clients to change the way they think about how you are contributing to their financial well-being.

 Discussion Question

What are some phrases or sayings you have used with clients in the past to stress the importance of following the advice you provide? What types of new language will you begin using, given your new awareness of the importance of language when you are the product?

Use Storytelling to Illustrate the Value of Financial Advice

Financial concepts can be complex and intimidating to our clients. It's easy to lose people when you begin talking about financial projections and "shop talk"—data and projections. Many of them are too embarrassed to admit they don't understand what you're talking about, so they can lose the value of your advice and become disengaged.

Storytelling is the key to explaining financial concepts in a way that engages people and helps them see how those concepts apply to their real-life situations.

Joe Jordan is an inspirational speaker, a behavioral finance expert, and the author of the award-winning book *Living a Life of Significance*. He believes storytelling is an integral part of building relationships with clients. He often says, "It's not a story of numbers; it's the number of stories."

One aspect of effective storytelling is to compare the point you are trying to make to another situation that people can relate to, from everyday life.

Here are five ways to demonstrate your value to clients by telling a story.

Storytelling Example 1: Compare Financial Advice with Personal Training

Here's an example. To simplify the concept of accountability for clients, you could compare financial planning with getting healthier. For example, you could tell your clients you've decided to live a healthier lifestyle. You started out by going for walks on nice days instead of sitting at your desk. Then you decided to keep a log of what you were eating so you could monitor how many calories you were taking in. And maybe you set a goal to work out at the gym (post-COVID, of course) three times a week.

Then you can say, "Even though those are great steps, though, I had a hard time sticking with my plan on my own."

So you decided to hire a professional trainer to meet you at the gym for training sessions. By waiting for you to show up, rain or shine, this person held you accountable. You were much more likely to go to the gym and do your workout.

Then you can explain how your trainer encouraged you and

taught you some important wisdom about the different types of exercise to do, the right balance of cardio work and strength training, and other tips. Working with that trainer is almost certain (if you follow his or her advice regularly) to enable you to improve your health.

Then you can tell your clients, "As your financial advisor, I'm going to be that trainer for you, that coach. I am going to teach you some important and valuable concepts. I'm also going to encourage you, adjust your plan as you experience life transitions, and answer the questions you have along the way."

Another effective storytelling approach is to provide examples of situations you have experienced or heard of with other clients—using fictitious names to protect their identities, of course. You can share with your clients, "I worked with someone who had a similar situation. Here's what happened." And then you can explain the appropriate action to take to work toward a positive outcome.

Those examples and scenarios, even if they're hypothetical, really resonate with people. They want to know about experiences you've had. They benefit from hearing about them. When they are engaged in an advice relationship with you, they benefit from all the education, experience, successes, mistakes, and interactions you have experienced with clients over the years.

Storytelling Example 2: Mention the "Real" Competition

Another phrase I like to use with clients is one we mentioned briefly a little earlier. I tell some of my clients, "My competition is death, old age, illness, and poverty, and my job is to get to my clients before the competition does."

Storytelling Example 3: Have a Clue for Just a Little Bit More Money

Another brief analogy that gets clients' attention is to ask them, "Would you rather make $250,000 a year and not have a clue if you're on track for your financial goals or to make $247,000 and have all the answers?"

The difference, of course, is a $3,000 financial planning fee.

Storytelling Example 4: Use a Simple Car Example

Just about everyone can relate to cars, and an effective way we've seen some advisors use storytelling to demonstrate their value to clients is to make a simple comparison between the wide range of vehicles available and the wide range of financial advisors who are in business.

Here's how this goes. You ask the client, "What kind of car do you drive?"

If the client mentions a vehicle on the upper end of value—maybe a Volvo, Mercedes, or Audi—you can respond by saying, "You know, there are cheaper cars. There are cars that cost a lot less than yours that will get you from point A to point B. But when you buy a Volvo or an Audi, you are paying more for the benefits and the features of a better car. And when we talk about how we work together in an ongoing advice relationship, what we're really doing is delivering a better car to you. We're not just doing the base transactions. We're not just getting from point A to point B."

Of course, if your client tells you he drives a thirty-year-old Chevrolet, this analogy won't work very well.

Storytelling Example #5: The Mechanic Metaphor

Here is a fifth story you can tell to help clients understand an advice-based practice:

Let's say your car is making a noise, and it's not running well. You take it into the garage, and the mechanic brings it into the repair bay. He pops open the hood and hooks up all kinds of diagnostic equipment. He starts the engine and begins listening carefully, observing what the dials and indicators are showing. In a few minutes, he is able to determine the car's alternator bearings are worn out. The alternator is not only no longer charging the battery; it is actually creating a drag on the engine's performance. So, after the mechanic installs a new alternator, he ensures the belt tension is correct, the whole system is charging properly, and the engine is running at capacity once again.

To solve the customer's issue, the mechanic used both his knowledge and his wisdom to apply the appropriate amount and type of labor to the solution.

So think parts and labor in your practice. In this metaphor, the car is the client's whole financial situation, and the alternator is a gap in that financial situation. You could compare this situation to a client not having lifetime income and the new alternator to purchasing an annuity. Without the mechanic's knowledge and wisdom to diagnose and solve the issue (like your financial advice), the problem could not be solved. The parts in the car metaphor are financial solutions, and the labor is the ability to diagnose the situation correctly and make sure the client's whole financial situation is working efficiently and effectively.

Storytelling is most effective when the stories you tell come from your heart, you tell them well, and they are highly relevant to what you and your clients are discussing. In your everyday life and work, look for examples of situations that will make compelling stories and make financial concepts easier to understand.

We want our clients to understand that one of the valuable benefits they get from working with us is that we serve as accountability partners. We not only customize financial plans based on their needs, wants, hopes, dreams, and fears; we shepherd them through the execution of that plan on a regular basis. We don't just hand them a huge binder and send them on their way.

Discussion Question

How skilled of a storyteller are you? What are some of the best stories you tell, or will tell, to clients to reinforce key concepts to them about living the best life possible with the money they have? What can you do to become a more skilled storyteller?

Participate in the Solution

Years ago, it was common for advisors to sit *across* a table or desk from their clients, closing transactions. In the financial-advice model, the visual image is a lot different. The client is sitting shoulder to shoulder with the advisor on the *same side of the table*. They're looking at the client's financial situation together. Clients bring their hard work, earnings, and revenue to the picture, and you bring knowledge, wisdom, and discipline. It's a partnership. Envision it differently. You are both participating in the solution.

How to Create an Exceptional Client Experience

When financial advice is your distinguishing factor, the goal is to offer an *exceptional client experience*. That term is subjective; it means something different to everyone.

But to get to the heart of what it means, I like to ask advisors, "How would I know I'm a top client in your practice?"

Once you segment your clients, it will be obvious to you how you serve them differently.

Leadership is taking someone to a place they would not have

gone on their own. Advisors do that for their clients, and leaders do it for advisors. This characterizes exceptional service.

 **Discussion Question**

What will you do to create exceptional client experiences in your Practice on Purpose? How will you enhance the frequency and quality of your communications? The way you greet clients and walk them out? What else?

CHAPTER 5

INVITING CLIENTS TO THE PERSONAL-ADVICE EXPERIENCE

Once you "go through the door" only you can go through, and focus your practice on ongoing advice relationships, it's time to invite your clients to be advice-based clients.

You can say to your clients, "We can work together a number of ways, but I'm going to invite you to consider that we engage in an ongoing, formal, comprehensive, advice relationship. The decision is yours."

We know the clients who agree to that model are more confident, more engaged, and make greater progress.

There is an element of fairness about this. Again, if you have clients who are in an ongoing-advice relationship for a fee, it's not really fair for you to provide the same services to clients who are *not* engaged at that level. So you have to be appropriate, fair, and professional.

Most Clients Welcome the Ongoing-Advice Model

One of the questions advisors ask me often is, "My practice is not currently advice-based. How do I transition my clients who are used to only paying commissions to an ongoing-advice relationship?"

When our advisors begin to transition their existing clients to an advice relationship, they typically feel fear and trepidation about it—and almost always, it's unfounded. Most clients welcome the ongoing-advice model.

In fact, many times, clients respond to this offer by saying, "I wondered if you would ever adopt this model. It's the way my CPA, attorney, and doctors provide their services."

Clients typically are less apprehensive about this arrangement than advisors. That's because they want to benefit from your knowledge. They want you to be dedicated to them in a comprehensive way.

I have witnessed advisors making this conversion. I am reminded of the phrase, "A good part of the journey is already behind you once you leave your front door." Once you make the commitment to yourself, you are well on your way. In one practice of 250 clients, 150 of them went to the advice model, and 100 elected to be service-only clients.

What to Say to Clients Who Prefer Not to Transition

But what if some of your clients don't want to transition to an ongoing-advice relationship? Some clients might tell you, "I don't like fees. I'm not doing that. Why do we have to change?"

You can respond by saying, "We don't. You can still be a client of our practice, and you'll get great service in all the ways we've worked with you in the past. Our team will take great care of everything we have in place. Ongoing financial advice is what most of my clients want in the future, and it's where we are taking the practice."

Once you gather the courage to have that conversation the first time, it will get easier.

How to Inspire Clients to Engage in the Planning Process

Draw on your strong sense of purpose—a strong sense of *why*—and you will have the courage to have this conversation with your existing clients.

New clients are pretty straightforward. Remember the three-tiered menu of service we discussed in chapter 4? *Show* that to your prospects, and describe the three levels of service you offer: holistic wealth management/ongoing advice, investment advisory (with a portfolio minimum), and transactional. Then ask, "How do you want to work together?" Or you could say, "Most clients who are in your situation work with us at this level."

I remember going on stewardship calls with my father for our church. He would prepare me in the car, saying, "You will want to help them come to a good place. Most want to give. They just don't know how much. And they don't want to be embarrassed or look foolish. They will be more nervous than we are. We have to guide them to have comfort in giving."

From those experiences, I learned this is also how we encourage our clients to adopt the ongoing-advice model. We have to guide them to have comfort in engaging with us at this level. There's nothing worse than having a financial-planning relationship that a client does not like or want. When that happens, they're pushing back all the time. For those clients, just let them be transactional. Take care of their product needs, if you choose to accommodate those clients. But you really want to work with clients who want to work with you in an advice relationship.

We don't want you to force clients into ongoing-advice relationships if they don't want that. However, you can lead clients to the best level of service by describing your compelling purpose and your desire to provide the best possible guidance to them on an ongoing basis.

You want to work with busy, successful people who, in turn, want to increase their probability of reaching desired outcomes.

Use Scripts to Enhance the Consistency of Your Messaging

When we coach advisors in adopting the financial-advice model, it helps them to have scripts to follow with existing clients.

At least in the beginning, when you are moving your practice to an advice-based model, scripts enable you to keep your messaging consistent and to choose effective language.

It's like a foreign language—the more you speak it, the more fluent you will become.

Advisors ask us for scripts often, so we are providing you with three sample scripts you can modify to your liking. The first one is to encourage existing clients to become ongoing-advice clients. The second one is to explain your focus on comprehensive advice to new clients. The third script is to explain the value of ongoing advice to clients who are navigating significant life events.

We hope you will revise these scripts to fit your situation and to sound like you. Practice them so you can deliver these concepts and messages to your clients in a natural way that doesn't sound like you're reading from a script.

1. Sample Script to Encourage Existing Clients to Become Ongoing-Advice Clients

I'd like to visit with you about the way we can work together as we move ahead. The reason is that I have a good portion of my clients asking for more services, asking more questions, and bringing me more complex situations. While I'm complimented by these requests, there are only so many hours in the week. I'm finding their lives have evolved to being more complex, and therefore, my practice needs to evolve to provide these services.

I want to determine what level of service interests you and matches your situation. We have three options: a service model based on work we have already done, a money-management relationship, or a comprehensive advice relationship that integrates all aspects of your financial world and drives us to reach your goals. Most people at your level of wealth and complexity engage in a comprehensive relationship where we cover the following topics [*show the menu of services*]. The decision is yours. In any case, you will remain part of our practice. Fortunately, I have an excellent team who will respond to those clients who have service requests. Clients in an advice relationship will continue to work with me and meet with me. We will have a defined service model and experience during the year.

I have found that clients who work with me in an advice relationship consider me the CFO of their household and the guardian of their financial future. With me, you are benefiting from literally thousands of client meetings, in which I have seen both smart and not-so-smart decisions regarding finances. My value to you is that I bring both knowledge and discipline to your financial situation to contribute to you reaching your goals. Most people will make a fortune in their lifetime. Without an advisor, they may not have anything to show for it in the end. Working in an advice relationship will mean that you will have a comprehensive, coordinated plan, and that money will be your servant, not your master.

How would you like to move forward?

It is a subtle pivot. You're not taking anything away from your existing clients. You're just adding value to those who want to work with you on an advice basis.

2. Sample Script to Explain Your Focus on Comprehensive Advice to New Clients

The next sample script is for you to use in describing your practice's focus on comprehensive advice to new clients.

Congratulations! You have a complex and successful life. You may have felt you had more discretionary income when you were in college than you do now. Part of our role in financial planning is to look at your cash flow, to look at money coming in, money going out, and actually know what's going where.

In the financial-planning process, we get our arms around the complexity of your successful life. You are working hard, you're time-strapped, and you're probably making good income, but let's make sure we know where the money is coming from and where the money is going.

A financial-planning approach will make that happen. Would that interest you?

The third sample script we're providing here is for you to use in describing the value of your financial advice to clients who are going through a life transition.

3. Sample Script to Explain the Value of Ongoing Advice to Clients Who Are Navigating Life Events

I've been studying my practice for the past couple of months. I realized there are at least three life events when financial advice is extremely important. The first one is going through a job change. It can be a promotion, getting a new job, or losing a job. The second one is marital changes. Financial advice is extremely important when someone is getting married or unmarried. The third one is retirement— approaching retirement, being newly retired, or being in the early stages of figuring out how you're going to recreate your paycheck in retirement.

The reason financial planning is so important during these three life events is that money and emotions are colliding. And sometimes when money and emotions collide, people don't make the best decisions. If you're in a financial-advice relationship, chances are, your advisor can lead you in navigating those life events so you make really good financial decisions—or the best ones you can make, given that you're going through a financially and emotionally vulnerable, and even chaotic, time.

If you know of anyone else in your social circles going through any one of those three events—hopefully not more than one at a time—maybe the best thing we can do is have them meet me as an advisor, so they can get assistance. While you may want to help them personally, introducing them to a financial-planning professional might be the best plan of action.

 **Discussion Question**

Of the three scripts just provided, select one to work with first. Modify it to fill in details about yourself and to sound like you. Commit to having this conversation with every client who falls into the appropriate category. Take notes on each client's reaction and response. Adjust the script along the way, as needed.

The Red-Car Story: Turn Casual Conversations into New Relationships

You don't have to acquire all your clients through formal means. Sometimes you can meet new clients in social situations that start out with a casual conversation. There is an art to creating an appointment from that kind of a situation. I call it "the lost art of conversation."

Wherever you are, keep your "antennae" up, and be aware that the person you just met at a holiday party, baseball game, or church function could be your next client. Based on your belief in yourself and the work you do, say to yourself often, "Let's see who I can help today."

I like to share my "red-car story" with advisors because it is a good example of how to transform a casual conversation into an invitation to be a part of your ongoing-advice practice.

One gorgeous spring day, I was in a little town in central Minnesota visiting an advisor at his office. I parked diagonally on the street because their streets are not designed for parallel parking. A man in his late fifties pulled up next to me in a brand-new, red Thunderbird convertible. He looked at me, and I looked at him and said, "Hey, nice car."

He said, "Yeah, I got this for retirement."

I replied, "That's quite the company you work for that you got a car like this for retirement."

He said, "Yeah" and laughed a little.

Then I asked him, "How did you know you could retire?"

His facial expression changed, and he said, "I got retired."

I could tell I had touched a nerve. He wasn't feeling good about where we were in the conversation. So I said, "There is a lot of that going around. It happens. But this is a really nice car."

He said, "My wife always wanted me to get a Thunderbird because I had a dream of having one when I was a teenager. I always looked up to them as a kid, and then Ford started coming out with them again."

We talked about cars for a minute. I said, "You mentioned that you 'got retired.' How do you know you can stay retired? I appreciate the car; it is great. But how do you know you can really retire?"

"Well, I really don't," he said.

I asked him, "Would you like to feel better about that decision? I work with financial advisors, and this is the kind of work we do. In fact, I just walked out of Mike's office. He is standing there in the lobby; I can see him."

The guy said, "I kind of know Mike."

"I want to introduce you to Mike," I said. "Would that be OK with you?"

I walked him in and introduced him to Mike, and we all engaged in some small talk. I said, "Hey, I love your car, and now you are in good hands." I left.

About a week later, I got a call from the advisor. He said, "Hey, that was an important meeting for both of us. The guy is actually in far better financial shape than he thought he was. It was great to meet him."

It all started with, "Hey, nice car." I didn't know where that conversation was going to go, but I am always aware that anyone I meet is a potential client for one of my advisors. If you approach every situation with that frame of mind, you can get good at turning those conversations into invitations to be a part of your uniquely qualified comprehensive-advice practice.

Everyone you meet is fighting a battle you do not know. Lighten their load, and make them more confident about their future.

Seek out the ideal clients we talked about earlier—the opinion-seeking and dependent clients who earn more than $150,000 of household income or are going to have this level of income. You deserve them, and they deserve you.

Discussion Question

Think of a time when you had a casual conversation with someone, and it turned into an opportunity. Now think of some occasions when you have missed the opportunity to turn casual conversations into discussions about changing someone's life for the better. What could you have done differently?

Follow the Doctor's Lead

Every spring, I used to get a horrific cold. Then one day, a buddy of mine said, "It might not be a cold. You might have allergies."

I thought, "I'm rough and tough, and I'm a guy. I don't have allergies." But I asked my general practitioner to refer me to an allergist, just in case. When I went to see her, she gave me a scratch test. She exposed the skin on my back to a wide variety of allergens, such as mold, pollen, and plants, to see if I had a reaction to any of them. She found out that I was allergic to several things and gave me a prescription for an allergy medication.

When she was finished, she asked me, "Has this been a good appointment for you? Do you think we got to the root of your problem?"

I said, "Yes, I think we did."

"You know, a lot of people walk around with allergies, and they have no idea that is what they have," she said. "I am new at this clinic and am establishing my practice. I would like to give you three business cards to carry in your wallet to give to people who may have symptoms similar to yours. You just said this has been helpful, and I can probably help some other people you know who have similar issues. Please carry these three business cards around and give them to people you know so that they can come see me. Better yet, if you let me know who they are, I will call them."

Think about that for a minute. This is a medical doctor. She worked extremely hard to get through med school, is very professional, and asked me to carry three of her business cards around. She was prospecting. I had a good appointment with her, so I was fine with recommending her. I thought, "If she can do it, why can't we do it?"

We can. Once you determine that a client is happy with your service, that is the perfect time to ask for a recommendation. It makes perfect sense to do so.

Prepare a Brief, Compelling Description of What You Do

Once you recognize your unique and significant value as a financial advisor, it's important for you to be able to describe your Practice on Purpose in a brief, compelling way.

This statement is often called an "elevator talk," which we believe is an overused term in our profession. This brief description, no more than one or two sentences, explains your life's work—and its value—to people quickly and concisely. This concept came from the idea of riding in an elevator with someone who asks you, "So, what do you do?" The elevator ride will last just a few seconds, so you don't have much time to explain what you do and how you can change people's lives.

Write your statement, refine it, and practice it until it sounds just right.

Here is one example of such a statement: "Well, my best clients tell me that what I do for them is make them feel confident about their financial situation. Would you like to meet some time so we can talk about how we do that? Would that interest you?"

Or you can say, "I work with busy, successful people to help them have the best life possible with the money they have. Would you like to meet sometime? I can share some ideas for how to make that happen for you. Would that interest you?"

 **Discussion Question**

> What is your brief, compelling description of what you do, now that you are transitioning to an advice-based practice? Write it down, practice it often, and keep track of when you say it to people you meet.

How to Respond when Someone Says, "I Already Have an Advisor"

Sometimes when you share what you do, even flawlessly, someone might say, "Well, I already have an advisor."

How do you respond to that?

One suggestion is to say confidently, "Well, many of my top clients had an advisor when I met them. When was the last time you heard from your advisor?"

Or you could say, "If you'd like a free second opinion, please contact me."

A bolder way of saying the same thing is, "That's great. Here's my card. If that job is ever open, I'd like to apply for it."

An advisor I was coaching at a different company came up with that last one. He told me, "You'd be amazed at how often you get a call when you tell people that." He explained that once people meet you and take a look at your business card, they'll think about it. They will realize they actually aren't completely happy with their current advisor. Maybe they haven't heard from their advisor in a while. Maybe it's just not a comfortable connection.

Whatever you say, the key is to be ready to answer that question. Don't let it catch you off-guard.

Why Giving Out a Business Card Is the End of the Contact

However, we do not recommend giving out business cards when you are at social or networking events and you meet someone who seems interested in what you do. Here's why.

When you give people your business card in a social situation, it puts them completely in charge of follow-up. You don't have their contact information, and if they toss your card in the garbage bin, that's the end of it. You don't really have a way to follow up.

Our suggestion is that you ask for the person's contact information instead. Or simply ask them to call you while you stand there so you will have their number. You also can share a contact. Most smartphones have a feature that allows you to share a contact.

This benefits you in a couple of ways.

First, it puts you in charge of the follow-up. Second, it signals that you're not just on the hunt, always prospecting, handing out business cards to everyone. It shows people you really didn't go there to have a conversation with them about what you do and what their interests are. You are just being social and enjoying the event.

Discussion Question

Are you in the habit of giving your business card to people when you first meet them? Role-play the strategy we have suggested here with someone, and then practice it in a social setting. Keep doing this until you get comfortable with it. To what extent do you see how asking other people for their contact information keeps you in control of the follow-up?

Embrace Your Unique Role in Managing Client Behavior

As advisors, we play a unique and critical role in our clients' lives. We are in the habit-formation, behavior-modification, intervention-specialist business. First and foremost, we encourage people to form the right habits around their goals and objectives. Then, on an ongoing basis, we ensure they are on the right track in reaching those important goals and objectives.

When we first meet with new clients, we can—comfortably, in a non-threatening way—intervene in their lives and encourage them to think about one of the biggest questions that are on most people's minds when it comes to their financial matters: "What is this world one day going to look like without me in it?"

That day is going to come for every single one of us.

As advisors, we acknowledge the fact there will come a day when we do not wake up. We are aware of how that will impact, in a financial way, the people we love, the causes we support, and the communities we live in. We have responsibilities and obligations to those people, causes, and communities. Once we're gone, we will no longer be here to support them financially. Have we left our finances in a position where everything will be OK?

It is our responsibility to lead our clients to this same critical understanding. If denial clouds their ability to accept the inevitable, it will lessen their ability to commit to working in partnership with you to implement the advice you provide.

The way we provide value is not by reaping a superior return on investments.

As you know, many people tend to make knee-jerk decisions based on emotions when the market starts to take a nosedive. They panic. And that never turns out well. What goes down will come back up.

A Vanguard study of more than 58,000 self-directed IRAs showed that investors who made material changes to their strategy even once in the five-year period from 2008 through 2012 suffered more than an 8 percent hit to the performance of their investments.[38]

Once you gain your clients' trust, they will likely listen to you when you remind them that pulling out of the market during a downturn is a bad idea. Left to their own devices, their panic can cost them dearly. It can take years to recover from even one bad move they make as a result of fear. You can prevent them from making mistakes like that. Your advice is priceless to them. They recognize it, and so can you.

Focusing on financial advice means partnering with your clients as they become ever-improving stewards of their money. The value you bring to them is priceless and multifaceted. Here are just a few of the many outcomes your leadership can help them to achieve:

- The benefit of the experience and knowledge you've gained through hundreds of meetings you have conducted, often with clients in their own professions or businesses

---

38. Ibid.

- A successful retirement

- A prepaid college education for their children

- Vacations, second homes, and travel

- A notable legacy through the creation of a foundation or charitable giving

- Financial dignity and financial choices

- Health, wealth, and happiness

Your clients deserve to benefit from your knowledge and experience. When common obstacles make that difficult, your unique quality of having "the heart of a social worker" comes into play again. You can move them past indecision and fear to action and progress.

Ask for Recommendations Regularly

Another key aspect of inviting clients to engage with you in ongoing-advice relationships is to ask your established clients for referrals—which we prefer to call "recommendations."

Earlier, we talked about the importance of the language we use as advisors. Asking for recommendations effectively, and regularly, is analogous to learning and knowing a foreign language. If we reach a certain level of fluency, let's say in German, we gain confidence the more we speak the language. On the other hand, if we don't speak German frequently, we lose confidence and become timid, and then we get worried about making a mistake and embarrassing ourselves, so we speak it less and less. Soon enough, we don't speak the new language at all. That's the way it is with the language we use to request recommendations.

Some advisors who start asking for recommendations are often quickly discouraged when they don't get immediate success, so they stop asking. If a Major League baseball player is hitting .300, that means he gets a hit only three of every ten times he is up to bat. He is out seven out of ten times. Babe Ruth, the legendary hitter, said, "Every strike brings me closer to the next home run."

Shrug off discouragement, and move on to the next opportunity. The more you ask for recommendations, the more you will receive.

The best recommendations are likely to come from your top clients. Once you have established relationships with the specific type of clients you want to work with, you can grow your practice exponentially by asking them to refer people they know to your practice. Chances are, they will know people who are like them in terms of demographics and income. Asking for recommendations when you are meeting with your best clients is one of the best return-on-investment strategies you can incorporate into your practice.

LinkedIn has proven to be an effective source of recommendations. Some of our advisors print out a list of professionals from LinkedIn and present the names to their clients. They say, "I am planning on calling on these folks. Would you be kind enough to eliminate any you think I should not call on?"

Keep in mind, though, that many people recommend downward. In other words, they will give you the names of people they know who make less money than they do. In that segment, you are a "deal" for them, but they are not ideal for you. Be aware of this, and try to encourage your clients to recommend you to people who are in a similar demographic group as they are. It helps to describe your menu of services and explain that you can do the most for clients who value what you do in the top service tier.

One of our advisors asks the question of his physician clients, "As a pediatrician, other than yourself, who in your opinion is the very best pediatrician in town?" Imagine the reaction of the latter when you call her with the compliment from her fellow practitioner! It might be the best one she hears all day.

Three Reasons Advisors Don't Get More Recommendations

There are three primary reasons advisors get fewer recommendations than they could:

- **They don't ask.** Remember, as Wayne Gretzky said, you miss 100 percent of the shots you don't take. I tell advisors to say to their clients, "I can't help people I don't meet."

- **They don't believe in themselves or in the value they provide.** Remember, when the advisor grows, the practice grows. As you gain confidence that you are delivering value, you will feel more comfortable about asking for recommendations. Believe that you have something of value because your client's family is going to benefit from your value more than yours will. That's a critical part of your belief system, and it should help you have the courage to ask people to join your practice.

- **They lack preparation.** They just haven't thought it through. They haven't practiced the language. They don't quite know when to ask for a recommendation, how to set the stage, or how to pivot in a way that is comfortable for the client.

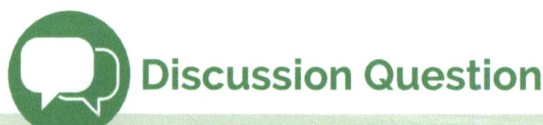 **Discussion Question**

How committed are you to asking for recommendations from your clients? If you were to commit to asking every client for a recommendation, how could that impact your practice, both quantitatively and qualitatively? Try it. Track the results, and determine the impact of this strategy.

Use the Family Tree Worksheet

This next strategy, which I call the "family tree worksheet," is one of the most impactful ideas I use when coaching advisors. I came up with this idea when I was a new advisor in Seattle. I had worked with a client for about two years. One day, he called to say he wanted to come by my office with a $2,000 IRA check, his annual deposit.

He said, "I want to bring my daughter. We would like to see your office." Because I was a junior advisor, my office was on the drab, parking-lot side of the building, not on the gorgeous Puget Sound side. That was good because I could see him pull up in a van. When the side door opened, a young girl got out, and she was in a wheelchair. Of course, I rallied pretty quickly and rushed to the front door to help them in.

I gave her a nice tour of our office; she was an absolutely delightful young lady. He told me she had cerebral palsy. It bothered me a lot that I had known this client for two years, yet I never knew he had a daughter in a wheelchair. I thought, "I just can't let that happen to me again."

A month later, I came across a family tree document, and I decided I would use it with all the important people I worked with.

I am natively curious about people's families. It makes the job more interesting. Knowing about a client's family not only gives you better insight into the client's life and priorities; it also helps you understand your clients' situations better. Numerous studies have revealed that one of the top reasons clients select a new advisor is because they felt their former advisor did not understand their situation. Using the family tree worksheet will help you understand your clients' situations much better.

The script goes something like this: "When you leave my office, you enter a world of people who are important to you. To be the best financial advisor I can for you, I would do a better job for you if I understood the world you go to after you leave my office. If you would, before our next meeting, complete this family tree diagram. It will be very helpful." Or you can mail it out before the next meeting. Once you see the completed worksheet, you will know if the client's parents are still living and if so, how old they are, as well as and who their siblings are and what they do for a living.

Once you have that information, you can ask questions like, "Who are your beneficiaries? Do you want to set up a 529 plan for your children?" There are many business implications for knowing the client's family and her relationships within her family. If your client says, "My sister works at 3M, and she just got promoted," you might circle back later and say, "You mentioned your sister. Is she working with an advisor? Would this type of conversation be helpful for her?" Or if your client's parents are aging, maybe one of them is struggling with memory issues. You might ask her if her parents should be meeting with her and her siblings. The discussion can go in a lot of directions.

We have seen people build almost their entire practice from knowing their key clients' family trees. Here is the family tree worksheet we now use at North Star:

Family Tree Worksheet

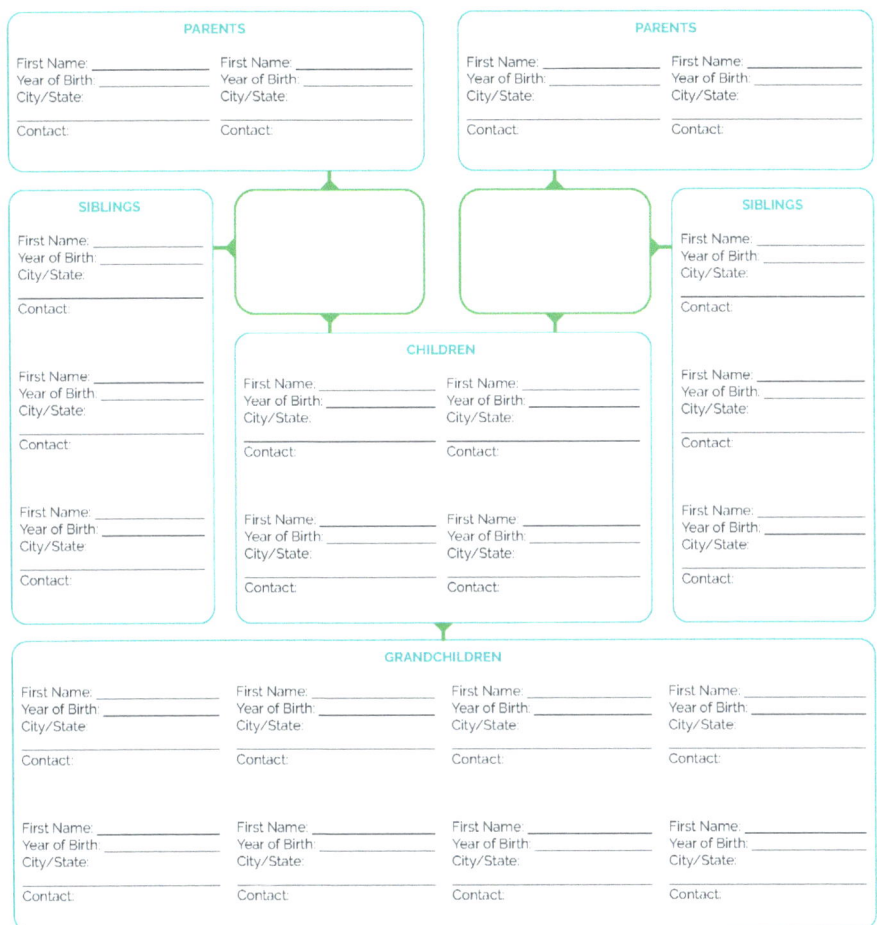

To what extent do you think the family tree strategy can lead you to a deeper understanding about your clients' situations? To what extent do you think it can lead you to work with your clients' family members?

Set Yourself Apart: Host Retirement Parties for Your Retiring Clients

When was the last time you attended a retirement party? I worked for a major financial services firm for ten years and went to one retirement party. They just don't happen anymore. People quit, get pushed out, or are given "special projects" and just shunted aside, with no proper send-off. As advisors, we can do something about that.

Several years ago, I attended a retirement party that one of my advisors hosted. He had conspired with his client's spouse to put together a gathering of his work friends. This was not a country club deal. This was a casual get-together at a VFW hall with sandwiches and beverages. This firm was one of those millionaire-next-door places—middle-class employment that made people millionaires over time.

The retiree's friends got up and toasted him, got him to blush, and cracked a few work jokes. No one from management was there. After about thirty minutes, the guest of honor got up and gave a tearful talk about his thirty years of work and the friends he made. As he wrapped up, he thanked his advisor who made this all happen and made him confident about his retirement. A big bear hug ensued, followed by a few introductions of interested pre-retirees.

How hard is it to honor a great career and just do the right thing, even if there were no recommendations? If the company cannot honor retiring team members, their advisors can do the job and recognize the good they do. This is an opportunity to honor clients in a unique, meaningful, and compelling manner.

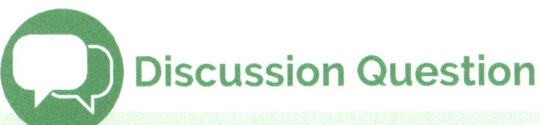

Discussion Question

Which of your clients are getting close to retirement? Consider hosting the celebration each one of them desires.

Now, in this chapter on inviting your clients to a personal-advice experience, we have shared some practical strategies, such as scripts to follow. In the next chapter, we discuss how to master additional elements of what we call "practice mechanics."

CHAPTER 6

MASTERING PRACTICE MECHANICS

We have made a strong case for *why* and *how* an advice-based practice benefits you and your clients significantly. Now let's move into the *what*—the nuts and bolts of building effective processes and strategies into your advice-based practice. We call this "practice mechanics."

Your client meetings make up a fundamental component of practice mechanics. We recommend the following guidelines for making your meetings useful to your clients and productive for both of you.

Make Your Client Meetings Purposeful

Meeting with prospects and clients regularly has always been the foundation of the profession we're in, and it isn't likely to change. Meetings are so important to building, retaining, and growing your practice that a lot of thought, planning, and intentionality needs to be built into each one. We want each meeting to be purposeful.

Too many advisors go to meetings without putting much thought into them. That is a missed opportunity because meetings are where your value proposition can be at its cutting edge. Use your meetings to move each client ahead in his or her financial situation by engaging with them systematically and repeatedly, in a purposeful way.

Accomplishing that begins with the preparation you do *before* the meeting.

Prepare an Agenda

A key factor in conducting purposeful meetings is to prepare an agenda in advance.

When you open the meeting, set the stage by asking what will make the meeting successful for them and what topics the client wants to cover.

An agenda typically covers the primary areas of financial advice. You can start out by saying, "How are things going with you? Has anything significant happened in your life since the last time we met? Here's what I plan to cover with you today."

Then hand your clients the agenda so you can go through it together. Ask them if they would like to add anything to the agenda. Take notes on the agenda during the meeting. When the meeting ends, both you and the client will have some action items. Let your clients know you will follow up with them about your progress on those tasks.

Also, be diligent about starting and ending your meetings on time. This is "time integrity" and reinforces your broader integrity— you do what you say you will do. Meetings shouldn't last longer than one hour. If you need more than an hour, schedule another meeting. Sometimes, we hear of advisors having three-hour meetings. That is fatiguing and excessive.

One of our other recommendations is to use a square room rather than a rectangular one. Use of the latter tends to lose those folks farthest from the speaker. Always end the meeting with a survey so you can receive feedback that will enable you to improve your future meetings. Ask whether additional information can be sent to them should they want it. Some advisors end the meeting with the offer of a group photo to be sent to attendees later. This guarantees contact information and can enhance the experience.

 **Discussion Question**

Do you use agendas in your meetings with clients? If not, consider doing so. Share it with clients before your meeting begins. Write down a sample agenda for a meeting. To what extent do you see how an agenda can streamline your client meetings?

Confirm Each Appointment with a "Pre-Call"

We also recommend doing what we refer to as a "pre-call."

Let's say I have an appointment with you next Tuesday. I will call you and probably leave you a voicemail saying, "Hey, Jerry, I'm looking forward to seeing you next Tuesday at two o'clock, I'm confirming the appointment. I want you to know that we are reviewing your file and looking at some of the work we did last time. I think we have some exciting things to talk about. You're making good progress. This will be a good meeting, and I look forward to seeing you. See you next Tuesday at two o'clock."

Now your client understands you're getting ready for that meeting, and you're taking it seriously. You're preparing a week or so in advance. You're not going to glance at his file for the first time while he or she is sitting in the waiting room, about to meet with you. That sounds funny, but unfortunately, it happens. And clients *know* when advisors do that.

We recommend making this call personally instead of having a team member do it.

Discussion Question

What will you say in your brief pre-calls?
Write down a sample script, and practice it.

Give Each Meeting a Theme

I read an article one time that said many clients equate meeting their financial advisor with going to the dentist to have a root canal. They dread it! The reasons vary, but many people don't understand our profession's data, jargon, and acronyms. Too many advisors forget that their clients don't speak our "language."

This is why it is critical to make all your meetings client-centric. Make it about them. Answer their questions. Address their concerns. Ask them to discuss what's going on in their lives, what they are looking forward to, and what concerns them. Then offer advice. Acknowledge when they have made progress. Make the meetings fun. People should enjoy the time they spend with you as they learn how to plan for a confident future.

We recommend that you assign a theme to your meetings to provide a deep dive on important topics while keeping the broader goals in mind. If there is no theme, it's easy for both you and the client to get bored. If that happens, the client is likely to disengage. Here are some ways to assign a theme to each meeting:

1. **The first meeting of the year might be a goal review.**
   You can use your notes from your previous contacts with the client to find out if her goals have changed. Always know every one of your client's top three financial goals. Keep this information visible and prominent in your clients' folders or in your contact management system. This information should be something you see every time

you have contact with a client. Everything you discuss, and every solution or action you recommend, needs to tie back to those three goals.

2. **The second meeting could be a portfolio and investment review, particularly around taxes, because by then, the client would have just completed them.** During that meeting, you can review her tax returns to determine the tax implications of her investments or protection products. You will keep those records as part of her client file.

3. **The third meeting could be a protection review.** Those meetings are often held in the early fall. Psychologically, that's a good time for a protection review because school is starting, winter's coming, and clients are focused on protecting themselves and their families.

4. **If there is a fourth contact, we call it an "integration meeting."** This is where the parts come together in a comprehensive plan—for example, planning a successful retirement. You want to find out if the client is getting closer to her goals since the last time you met. What has she accomplished? Does she feel good about the work she has done with your guidance? At this point, it might be the time to re-establish your advice fee if you are working with advice clients.

Document the Meeting Content

After you meet with clients, write them a follow-up note. If they are advice clients, document the advice you gave them. Depending on your company's compliance requirements, you might be required to mail the client a letter. Sometimes an email is acceptable.

The purpose of this step is quality control, to keep things moving forward. There's nothing more annoying—for your client, especially—than covering the same topics twice because you forgot you already discussed something in the previous meeting.

Before you begin your call or your meeting, you can look over the previous meeting's summary, and you're off and running to what comes next. You don't end up rehashing what happened before. It enables you to be highly productive and future-facing. You might have fifty or a hundred other client meetings after you meet with a client. By documenting key points from your meetings, you don't have to try to remember them when you meet again.

This shows your clients you're on top of their situations and following through with what you told them you would do.

Clients and prospects are hungry for someone to take an interest in their financial future and an authentic interest in them. Again, people are drowning in financial noise and starved for specific knowledge and wisdom.

Our definition of *leadership* is to take people to a place they would not have gone on their own and leave them better than you found them. Your clients need—and expect— this level of leadership from you. It is the distinguishing factor that enables you to lead people to live the best lives possible with the money they have.

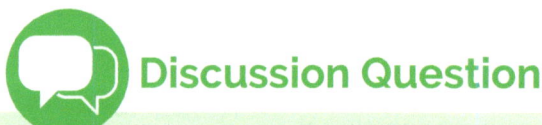 **Discussion Question**

How diligent have you been about documenting, and then summarizing, key points discussed and decided during your client meetings? Have you ever inadvertently repeated information or forgotten a detail because you did not take good notes? If you could improve in this area, how will you go about documenting your meetings?

Always Schedule the Next Meeting

No client should leave your office without scheduling the next meeting. Make it informal. Everyone carries a phone. Ask them to take out their phone, look at their calendar, and suggest a time a few months away that will work for them.

Getting this appointment on the books now does a lot of things for both of you. First, it eliminates the hassle of trying to schedule a call. We're all busy. You don't want to have to hunt down a client and play phone tag just to get an appointment on the calendar. Also, when clients schedule appointments, they tend to work harder to meet the commitment..

But if your clients have no clue when they're going to see you next, or there's no certainty that you even have an ongoing-advice relationship with them, they are vulnerable. It also erodes the goal-achievement momentum.

Scheduling the next meeting is good positioning for you. If another advisor approaches your client, it provides protection for you because the client feels secure, knowing that meeting is on the calendar. If your clients don't have a clue when they're going to see you next, it makes them somewhat vulnerable to taking a call from another advisor or saying, "Gee, I don't know when I'm going to meet with my advisor next." You want them to be able to say with confidence, "My advisor has it covered and is on top of my situation. I have a meeting scheduled with my advisor in two months."
Plus, they can be preparing questions to ask you during that next meeting.

Having that next call scheduled keeps the client–advisor relationship tight.

Discussion Question

In the past, how often did you schedule the next meeting when you finished meeting with a client? Make it standard procedure. Keep track of your progress in this area, and strive to *always* schedule that next meeting before you leave a client meeting.

Pay Equal Attention to Everyone in a Group

Too many times, when advisors work with couples, they address one client more than the other. For example, if the woman seems to be the spouse who makes the financial decisions, it's easy to let her husband sit back and listen, without participating. It's more common, though, for the husband to be the one asking all the questions, while the wife sits back without participating.

This is unacceptable. Everyone you work with needs to understand their financial situation and the impact of the decisions they make.

It's quite common for a woman to consider an advisor to be her husband's advisor, not hers. That is most likely because many advisors work harder at forming a bond with male clients than with those clients' wives.

We have a huge opportunity in this profession to make the client experience better for women. According to a multi-year national study of women clients completed by New York Life Investments, women felt that financial advisors ignored them and made little effort to understand or solve their financial problems.[39]

39. "Women Feel Ignored by Advisors, Study Says," R. J. Shook, *Forbes*, August 7, 2020, https://www.forbes.com/sites/rjshook/2020/08/07/woman-feel-ignored-by-advisors-study-says/.

Half of those surveyed said their financial advisor was incapable of connecting with them on a personal level by taking time to understand their specific needs. Forty percent said advisors treat women differently, often ignoring or dismissing what they have to say. And 62 percent of women said they have unique investment needs, yet financial advisors don't understand those needs.[40]

When widows change advisors, that tells us they were not in engaged-advice relationships with their advisors, which is the topic of chapter 3. Good advisors will engage everyone in the family in the conversation about financial health. They will even bring the client's children and parents into the picture, as well as the client's CPA and attorney. Smart advisors take a comprehensive view of their clients' situations because they're in an advice relationship.

A technique that is helpful in all client meetings is to think the people in front of you have invisible signs around their necks that say, "Make me feel important." All people—regardless of their occupation, education, net worth, dreams, and hopes—deserve to be treated with respect and dignity. This is doubly true when they have come to you and opened up about a subject that is so intimate and important to them and their families—their finances.

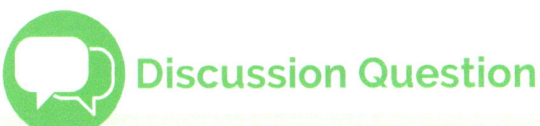 **Discussion Question**

When you work with couples, to what extent do you know and understand both parties' goals, concerns, dreams, fears, and financial situation? If you think you can improve in this area, what will you do to begin giving both parties equal time, energy, and attention?

_____

40. Ibid.

Nurture the Client Relationship

Nurturing client relationships is an area many advisors overlook today because of the "hunting" mindset so many of them bring into the career. We see too many missed opportunities for advisors to connect with clients and create an exceptional experience for them. This important aspect of an advisor's practice can be taken care of so easily with competent team members and the technology we have today.

Your team members can send your clients timely, relevant information with a couple strokes of the computer keyboard. It's a matter of being aware that you can be highly visible to your clients and having a system in place to ensure that you "touch" your clients regularly with some type of communication.

One way to nurture a client relationship is to compliment your clients on their progress. Notice when they're doing something well, and give them "tough love" when they're not.

We often talk about the "richness" of communication. Face-to-face communication is rich and warm. You get to see your clients, shake hands with them, and communicate while you're both in the same environment. Handwritten notes are a fairly rich mode of communication. At the other end of the spectrum—the cold and unrich side—are the less personal modes of communication like email. Having a team member call a client on your behalf is somewhere on that continuum.

To nurture client relationships, know what level of richness you need for what you're trying to accomplish. If you are confirming a meeting, an email is fine. If you're trying to convince a client to save money or buy a range of insurance products, that needs to be rich, so it needs to be a face-to-face meeting.

The key is to "touch" your clients many times throughout the year, with all types of communication. You can send them holiday cards, pictures of your family, pictures of your team, handwritten notes, and links to online articles they might enjoy. Many of our advisors email newsletters to their clients regularly. There are a lot of things you can do with technology and the Internet now, including email updates.

We encourage advisors to have a "hot" list of clients who should receive a call when certain things happen, such as if the market drops 100 points in one day. Or, let's say something happens overseas that you know might affect a client. You can call him and say, "Hey, I know you have a lot of holdings in Greece. I'm calling to let you know that I'm aware of what's going on. I looked at your portfolio, and I don't recommend that you make any moves at this point. I'll let you know if that changes." When you make it a point to communicate with your clients at that level, you are developing a highly nurtured relationship.

It's important to know what each client likes. Some people enjoy getting candy baskets at Christmas. Others couldn't care less and think you're wasting your money. The better you know your clients, the better you can nurture your relationship with them.

One of our advisors calls each man in his practice about a week before that client's wedding anniversary to remind him that it's coming up.

If you know your clients have saved money to go on a nice trip, why not have a bottle of champagne waiting for them when they arrive at their hotel? You can attach a note to it that says, "Congratulations on your trip!"

Some advisors will send to a client a book they know will interest them. They will mail it with a note that says, "I saw this in a bookstore the other day and thought you might like it." There are rules about how much money you can spend on gifts, but you can do small things.

Each effort you make to connect with a client matters. These "touches" add up and contribute to an exceptional client experience, which, in turn, will result in client satisfaction and loyalty, more recommendations, greater personal satisfaction for you, and growth in your practice.

What system will you put in place to "touch" your clients many times throughout the year, with all types of communication? What types of communication will you send? Which of your clients will you add to a "hot list" of those who will receive communications from your practice about important market-related developments?

Know How Your Clients Are Paid

As you build your advice-based practice, remind your clients that you are their financial CEO, and you've got their backs all the time. Even if you are meeting with them formally only a few times each year, let them know you are aware of events that are important in their lives. Follow up with them about topics you've discussed. "Touch" them often to let them know you have an eye on their situations.

One way to add value is to know how every client is paid, whether it's a paycheck from a company, from a small business, or something else. Anticipate salary increases to guide your clients in managing that newly acquired money.

Here is an example. Maybe your client shared with you she was going to have a salary review in two months. This is a great opportunity to connect with her. If she gets a salary increase, bonus, or stock options, that's new money. Talk with her about how to make at least some of that increase a part of her overall financial plan. Most people spend new money. With advice from you, the advisor, though, you can encourage them to save most of the new money and maybe spend a little.

Then, a year later, you can show your client how that money grew, and that will again reinforce your value in her eyes.

Here's another example. Let's say it's November, and you are working with clients to select their enrollment in employee benefits with their employers. Ask them which benefits they are thinking about enrolling in, and ask if they have questions. Maybe they are thinking about participating in a health savings account, or HSA. Offer advice on how they can integrate that into their financial plan. Explain how that plan could benefit them tax-wise. That's a valuable service.

This is true leadership. You are *anticipating* a situation instead of *reacting* to it or waiting for your client to ask you about it.

Some clients think the advisor is going to take away all their fun. In reality, we want them to save *and* have fun. We want them to know, "The money you save will still be your money. Yet a year from now, or five, or thirty years from now, not only will it still be your money; that money will have friends. It will have grown."

That phobia does exist among some clients. They resist having a financial advisor hold them accountable. They think we are going to tell them they can't buy a new car or go golfing or something. Of course, we want our clients to have fun, yet part of our value is encouraging them to have some discipline to save. And when they get an increase, it will be helpful for them to put part of it toward their financial plan.

Discussion Question

How familiar are you with the ways in which your clients get paid for the work they do? Make this an action item. Find out this information, explain to your clients why you're asking for it, and add it to your CRM. Then follow up with every client about optimizing the use of "new" money when opportunities arise.

Meeting Frequency

The ideal frequency of client meetings has changed over the years.

In the 1960s and 1970s, the model was to call on prospects and clients at their homes. Virtually all meetings were face-to-face, and an advisor's client base was usually confined to those who lived a relatively short distance away. Knocking on doors in an affluent neighborhood was not uncommon.

Moving into the 1990s, there was a trend to meet at the advisor's office. An advisor could see more clients in a day, and it was analogous to how a CPA, doctor, or attorney would meet with clients. It assured confidentiality and that all the necessary paperwork was close and convenient. A comparison with dentist-office operations also increased efficiency and effectiveness.

It was common to alternate in-person visits with phone conferences. Advisors found their ideal clients were often a busy working couple with work as well as day-care or pet responsibilities. Meeting in person every time was not ideal or necessary.

Then our unwelcome visitor—COVID-19—appeared. In March

2020, it all changed and, in many ways, we're not returning to how we interacted with clients before. Most advisors went to a phone call or one of the video conferencing capabilities, such as Zoom, to engage with their clients. There was a significant pivot, and it worked. Clients needed and wanted the contact. Technology made this happen.

Technology streamlined our operations again when it became possible to take a picture of a check with your phone and have it deposited,. The use of digital signatures also made in-person contact less necessary. In eighteen months, the way we work with clients regarding their personal financial matters changed more than in the previous fifty years. These are exciting times, and there is a silver lining to the pandemic.

Earlier, we discussed segmentation and how it matches increased meeting frequency. There is a correlation between your segments and the number of personal contacts you have in a year. You can meet with your top-segment clients three to four times a year via a combination of phone, in-person, and digital interactions.

Be the leader here—do not let your clients drift or become disengaged. In the past, we've been able to "hide" behind email when there needs to be personal touch. There is a risk that digital can become the new email.

It's important to obtain input from all your clients regarding how they want to interact, yet it's up to you to keep the engagement tight. Be the one who defines and leads with your client-service model, or else your clients will end up doing so. When you provide leadership, your Practice on Purpose will stay true to its mission— for your clients and for you.

Meeting Method

The COVID-19 pandemic changed the way we work, and I think those changes will stick around for the foreseeable future.

When advisors conducted all their meetings in person, their

client base consisted of people who lived in their immediate geographic area. But now that Zoom meetings have become the norm, we can meet with anyone, anywhere. Today, some of our advisors are working effectively with clients they've never met face-to-face. This has opened up advisors' markets and improved efficiency enormously.

Compliment Your Clients on Their Progress

As advisors, we play a unique role in our clients' lives. Most people have no one who knows anything about their financial situation except for their financial advisor. That gives us a unique opportunity to reinforce their success and celebrate their progress.

Imagine how great your clients will feel when you tell them, "You know, I work with a lot of different clients. I want to point out that you and your spouse have done really well, and I want you to celebrate how well you have built your careers, your family environment, your vacations, and the travel you do. You have a really good life, and I just want to compliment you, congratulate you, and express that it's really a privilege for me to be part of your life. I also want to share with you that I think I'm in a unique position to tell you you're doing really well."

We should not be shy about sharing these sentiments with our clients. It gives us an opportunity to focus on family life, express gratitude, recognize their well-being, and celebrate the progress they have made in working hard to develop good habits that will enhance their future.

Prepare Your Practice for the Winter

Here in the Midwest, we have sure signs that winter is coming. The State Fair is over, children are back in school, sprinkler systems are being blown out, boats are being taken in, shrubs are trimmed back to handle the snow, patio furniture is moved into basements, and jackets are set out.

The approach of winter also indicates it's time to perform some key practice-management activities. For a group I coach, we have been discussing the following four actions to prepare for winter.

1. Connect with Clients You Need to See by Year-End

Virtually all advisors at North Star have segmented their clients based on criteria meaningful to the advisor—usually by revenue, assets, type of financial-planning relationship, potential, or how engaged they are with the advisor. This is a great time to review your segments to determine who needs to be seen before the end of the year.

The year can get away from you and your clients. We don't want to miss anyone who needs contact and engagement. It's easy to overlook key clients who are not demanding yet are important. So don't let the year end without seeing everyone who needs to be seen. This is double-important for clients who have year-end bonuses coming. We want to get in front of them to make sure some of their bonus money goes toward their financial plans.

2. Conduct a Six-Month Look-Back

I once met the top advisor at Prudential. She was down-to-earth and had a fantastic practice outside Ann Arbor, Michigan. We were waiting at the Buffalo airport in the dead of winter after we both spoke at a local conference. She had many tips on running a great practice, yet one of them really stuck with me.

Each fall, she would block out a day and go back over all her appointments from the prior six months. What she was looking for were second- and third-level topics from those meetings that did not happen because they worked on the number-one issue first. She was able to address those lower-priority topics, demonstrate follow-up to her clients, and increase revenue at the same time. She said one activity would often put her over the top on convention recognition and other measures that required an extra push. Everybody won.

Also identify who is turning 65 or retired and is now on Medicare. Should your Medicare team contact those clients?

We are also having great success with property and casualty (P&C) audits with affluent clients. This often results in better coverage with better companies, and half the time, we can save them money. Gather their declaration pages from the cover of each policy, and have your P&C team review them. Discovering the number of clients who do not have umbrella policies has been an eye-opener.

3. Make January 2nd a Great Day

How would you like to walk into your office on January 2nd and have a full calendar for the next ninety days with your top clients and prospects? You can if, in the fall, you look at your client segmentation and determine who needs to be scheduled in November/December to be seen in the first quarter.

If you wait until January to start that scheduling, you are already behind for the year. If your top clients know they are scheduled, they will have the confidence that you are on top of their situation. If a competitor contacts them, they will be less likely to take the bait.

We also know your first quarter can often make the year. If you get off to a fast start, it tends to create energy for the year. It's not about working hard; it's about working on the right things. Seeing the clients who represent 80 percent of your revenue in the first ninety days is working on the right stuff.

4. Leverage the Holiday Spirit to Meet New People

Many advisors consider the time between Thanksgiving and New Year's as a slow or dead time of the year. Yet some advisors view that time of a year as a period of elevated spirits, a bit more time flexibility, and more awareness about the importance of family and friends.

It can be a great time to turn a casual conversation into an appointment. We want to be classy and respectful about how we approach people, yet when you see families enjoying the holidays, consider the positive impact you can have on the lives of those family members. Their families benefit far more than your family when they become your clients. Who are we not to offer that gift?

Consider building these and other activities into your practice mechanics, and you will likely increase your impact.

 **Discussion Question**

Of the four ideas just suggested for preparing your practice and clients for the winter, which one appeals to you the most? Why? How will you begin implementing that strategy into your interactions with clients?

Understand How Much Your Clients Benefit from Working with You

We once hired an etiquette coach to meet with our advisors who were hosting seminars. The coach provided tips on how to behave in a room and introduce people to each other. It helped a lot.

The stronger your social skills, confidence, and ability to communicate your value, the better you will be at attracting the right clients.

An important question to ask yourself, no matter how long you've been in this profession, is "Whose family benefits more by becoming my client? Does my family benefit more, or do my clients' families?" The answer is that you will benefit a little, but your clients will benefit much more. Acknowledging that fact, having that conviction, will arm you with a strong value proposition.

In his book *The Good That Financial Advisors Do*, Dan Sullivan lists compelling benefits advisors provide to clients in the twenty-first century. If you need a good reminder about the value you bring to the table, read what he has to say.

Once you determine who you are as a person first and then as an advisor—in other words, once you define your value proposition—you will begin to attract like-minded people who have similar political or life philosophies. Your practice will reflect your central purpose in life and the purpose of your practice.

Now that we have covered practical strategies for streamlining your practice *mechanics*, let's discuss strategies for optimizing your practice *economics*.

CHAPTER 7

MASTERING PRACTICE ECONOMICS

For decades, we have let our products pay us for the financial advice we give. The world is changing rapidly.

If you are transitioning to an advice-based practice, chances are, you will have an opportunity to change the way and/or the amount you charge for your services. "Practice economics" is an important aspect of running your practice in a way that provides value for your clients *and* compensates you for what you're worth.

If you have professional designations, think of the hours you invested in learning, studying, and applying the concepts you learned in those educational programs. That is valuable to your clients. Not everyone has that knowledge. Now think about all the meetings you've had over the years and the financial plans you have developed for clients. That experience is extremely valuable. It is the foundation of the saying, "If I do a job in thirty minutes, it's because of all the experience I have gained through the years. You owe me for the years, not the minutes."

And then, when you combine your unique knowledge and experience with your personal understanding of each individual client's situation, goals, dreams, and fears, again, you become invaluable to them—irreplaceable. The longer you have known your clients, the more meetings you've had with them over the years, and the more you understand what they are trying to accomplish, the more irreplaceable you are.

If you specialize in a given market, think of your ability to share the best practices of others in the same profession with each client within that group.

Who Is a Profitable Client?

We have already postulated that when you value your advice, you will have the courage to charge what you are worth. When you value your advice, you will have the courage to charge appropriately for its economic value. To do this, it's important to know what and who constitutes a profitable client.

To discover this key piece of information, you first need to know what it costs you to have a client. If you were to add up your time, your staff members' time, your physical office space, your licensing fees, and all the other costs of doing business, what would that number be?

Some advisors have written books on the topic of how to determine the ideal cost structure of your practice. Once you know that number, then you can determine what a "profitable client" is for your practice. Keep this number in mind as you decide who your target market is.

The diagram shown next illustrates the structure of a profitable client-service model.

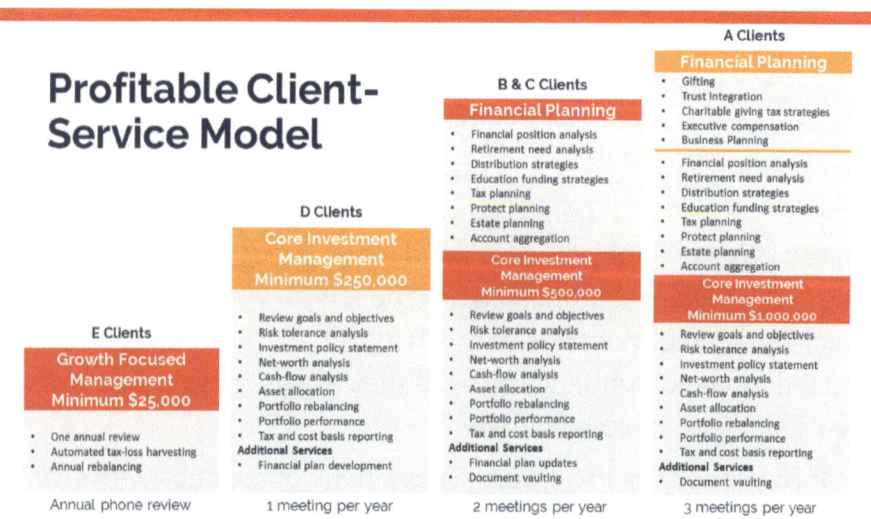

Discussion Question

> Keeping in mind our earlier discussion about segmenting clients, and after reviewing this "Profitable Client Service Model" diagram, what ideas to you have for determining the ideal cost structure for your practice?

The Interplay Between Investment Advisory (AUM) and Advice Fees

In 2021, North Star Resource Group brought in more than $7 million in planning fees involving 3,500 households. Yet we are prouder of the case count than we are the fees because that means we have provided 3,500 families with a plan at our firm. It's a great feeling to know we are changing the lives of these 3,500 families and businesses.

One of our advisors, Jane, recently began offering financial planning for a fee. She now has 125 cases, 125 plans, and $280,000 of revenue from those plans. That's an additional source of revenue she never had, but more important, she has 125 very engaged clients who are getting some level of a formal plan with her every year.

The persistency of ongoing fees for future advice is key. It's a little bit of a sale. Every year, you have to remind your clients why they're paying a fee, what's in it for them, and how your ongoing advice benefits them and their families.

We encourage you to reduce your IA fees and backfill with financial advice. With this approach, you will be super-competitive on the IA side, yet you will be paid appropriately for the comprehensive advice and knowledge you're providing on the planning side.

Recurring/Annually Renewing Fees or Periodic Fees?

Advisors often ask whether they should charge recurring/annually renewing fees or periodic fees.

There are certainly situations in which a one-time fee or periodic fee is warranted and is the right thing to do for the client. However, in most cases, we think recurring/annually renewing fees lead to more progress and contribute to higher goal achievement.

It's a little bit like medical insurance. You don't know what year you're going to get really sick, or what year you're going to not need the insurance, but you always want to have it. It's the same with recurring/annually renewing advice. Some years, you will need to do a lot of work with a client, such as when one of those significant life experiences arises.

During that period, frankly, your fee may be too low that year for the work you did. Yet another year, it might be pretty much cruise-control. It all evens out.

Also, charging recurring/annually renewing fees gives your clients permission to call you and involve you because they know you are essentially in a relationship with them. You want them to call you when they have questions. You want them, their spouse, and anyone in their family to reach out to you because they know you are in an ongoing-advice relationship with them. Not only is that OK; it's invited. This sends a message to them that they are getting significant value by engaging with you at this level. Some people refer to this as "concierge service."

What Determines Pricing?

"How much do you charge?" is a question I get often. Many factors determine what your appropriate pricing is, including your client relationships; the services you provide; compliance; the cost structure of your practice; and your clients' assets, net worth, and financial complexity.

What to charge your clients can be categorized in a four-part grid:

Price & Value Matrix

High **PRICE** **Low**	**Lose clients**	**Mature practice featuring exchange of best efforts**
	Transaction, not a relationship	**Lose practice; advisor is overworked and underpaid**
	Low **VALUE** High	

We have price on the vertical axis and value on the horizontal axis. As you can see, there are four potential scenarios of what you will offer:

1. **Low price and low value**—This is the level of service that is transactional. In this scenario, your clients are not advice clients.

2. **Low price and high value**—In this scenario, you're delivering value all over the place. You are providing great value, but you're not charging very much because you don't accept your true value, or you are rationalizing that you are making enough compensation on the investment side, or some other reason. It's just not sustainable. In this scenario, you could lose your practice. You are

145

overworked and underpaid. We see this too often.

3. **High price and low value**—In this scenario, you charge a really high price, but you are not doing very much for that price. In that scenario, you're going to lose clients. They will know they are not getting much for their money, and they will eventually leave.

4. **High price and high value**—This is the best of both worlds and the hallmark of a mature practice. In this scenario, you recognize your worth and charge for it. You are exchanging your best effort for compensation you deserve. Clients also wins when they get high value for the appropriate fee.

Your pricing will vary according to the number of years you've been in the business and your credentials. Client factors will impact your pricing, too, including how complex is the client's financial situation. Higher complexity requires more expertise and more time, and hence a larger fee.

Now, although your pricing needs to be *fair*, it won't be *equal*—it won't be the same for every client. You will not charge the same fee to work with a single earner, a dual-income household, a business owner, a practicing physician, and a corporate executive. Your pricing structure needs to make sense and have a certain element of consistency to it. Imagine if all your clients were to get together at a picnic and compared the fees they pay—would they make sense to everybody?

The sample monthly financial planning fee grid shown below illustrates how advisor capability and client complexity affect the amount you might charge various categories of clients.

Sample Financial Planning Fee Grid

Client Complexity					
		Single Earner	Dual Household	Dual w/ Children	Business Owner	Practicing Physician or Corporate Executive
Advisor Capability	Mentored advisor	$2,400	$3,600	$4,800	$6,000	$12,000
	5 years of experience	$2,400	$3,600	$4,800	$6,000	$12,000
	10 years of experience	$4,800	$4,800	$6,000	$7,200	$12,000
	CFP® advisor	$6,000	$7,200	$8,400	$9,600	$12,000

Source: North Star Financial Data 2022

Be deliberate about your pricing model. If you're not in charge of your clients' service model, the clients are in charge. *You* want to be in charge. Advisors who are not deliberate and thoughtful about this important aspect of their practices often lose enthusiasm about the career.

You Are Fully Compensated for Your Value in a Fee World

When advisors are in the commission world, their compensation is tied to what manufacturers want it to be. The value is baked into the features and benefits of that product. Think of an annuity or life insurance product—even a mutual fund or municipal bond. The pricing and value are predetermined and prescribed. The value the advisor brings to the picture is partially the access to the product. The advisors are representing the product companies to the clients. The commission value restrains their ability to realize their full value.

Yet in the fee world, advisors can price for their *full* value. This can be in the form of an asset-management fee or a financial-advice fee. Advisors set their compensation and are compelled to deliver on their value to their clients.

We all know the phrase, "In the absence of value, price is an issue." The corollary is even more important: "In the presence of supreme value, price is not an issue." We are reminded of the oatmeal story from chapter 1 in this book, about becoming indispensable to your clients. The value you bring to your clients' experience and to their financial outcomes is almost beyond price. The responsibility then falls on you, the advisor, to articulate the value you bring to your clients and then to have the courage to charge appropriately for this value.

With this approach, advisors can try to build their own practices, or they can form a strategic partnership with a robust team of specialists in a healthy and high-performance culture. This, as we illustrated in the preface, "The World Is Becoming North Star," is our promise to our advisors and their clients. Your value as an advisor is enhanced by being part of North Star. In turn, our value is enhanced by having partnered advisors.

This sets you free to be your own person and to be your own professional. What a refreshing model for both advisors and clients!

What if There Were No Product Compensation?

Here is a good exercise for you to do as an advisor. Consider if there were no product sales, no product compensation at all, and a prospect or client asked you, "How much would you charge me to do a financial plan with no implementation?"

Considering this scenario makes a clear distinction between products and planning. Ask yourself, "What would I do if I were only going to work on a financial plan?" Periodically, clients and prospects ask this question. It encourages you to think about the value of your time and advice.

How much time are you actually going to devote to gathering data, producing a plan, meeting with the client, considering various alternatives, and putting recommendations in place? If that were the only compensation you would receive, what would you charge?

How Much Are You Worth per Hour?

Another good exercise to do is to ask those same questions to determine what you are worth *per hour*.

There are 2,080 working hours in a year. What is the take-home compensation you want for the year? Let's say you decide your skills, experience, knowledge, wisdom, and abilities are worth $750,000 per year in take-home compensation.

The next question is, what does your gross income have to be to take home $750,000? It's a simple calculation: 2,080 hours divided by $750,000 comes to $360.58 per hour. This is the hourly rate you deserve, based on the value you provide.

Knowing this vital fact might make you think twice about spending time on activities like scheduling meetings and making copies. When you catch yourself doing those things, remind yourself, "This is not $360-an-hour activity. This is something lower."

That will get you to start thinking about what type of staff you need—who should be doing what in your practice. The highest-value activities for you to focus on are prospecting for new clients and meeting with your top clients.

Keep that number front of mind as you are working to establish your ideal practice economics.

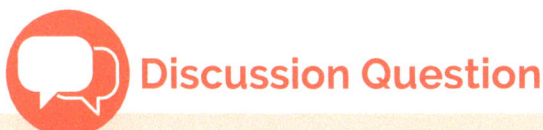 **Discussion Question**

Using the calculation above, determine what you are worth per hour. How close is that to what you have been charging? What can you do differently to focus more on the higher-level work? Which tasks will you delegate, and to whom?

Identify Your Top Priorities

We have produced a deck of fifty-two cards called "Drive." On each card is printed a key activity that advisors focus on in their practices. We developed the cards from the results of a survey one of our interns conducted with our top fifty advisors at North Star. It is basically an exercise in ranking your top priorities.

At a recent Platinum Study Group meeting, we had our top a advisors do a forced ranking to isolate the top five activities that are best done only by them. Here are the five highest-yield activities best done by advisors:

1. Meeting with top long-term clients
2. Working with clients to prioritize goals
3. Presenting comprehensive financial plans
4. Asking for recommendations or introductions
5. Preparing case analyses and recommendations

Advisors find this resource highly useful in identifying their top priorities.

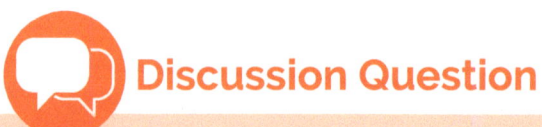

Discussion Question

Reviewing the five highest-yield advisor activities listed above, how well do those align with your highest priorities? What tasks are you spending time on now that prevent you from focusing on higher-impact activities?

Value of Advice Fee Structure

Roy T. Diliberto, ChFC®, CFP®, is the founder of RTD Financial in Philadelphia. He has written two great books about financial planning (included in the "Suggested Reading" appendix). He often uses a great comparison between financial planning and the medical services provided by a doctor.

The doctor tells someone, "If you hire me as your physician, I will treat all your illnesses. I will help you with dieting, recommend preventive care, prescribe drugs, monitor your progress, refer you to competent specialists when needed, and be available for questions. In short, I'll be your comprehensive medical advisor."

The patient asks, "How much is this going to cost?"

The doctor replies, "Well, all you have to do is buy drugs from me."

Let that sink in for a second. What seems to be the most important thing the physician does? Selling drugs. Are you concerned the physician will be compelled to sell you drugs? Are you worried that you may not need those drugs? What would happen if you paid the doctor a retainer for the other services and bought the drugs on your own?

Diliberto's point is, why should financial planning be any different? Why do we earn the most from *commodities* we offer instead of the most valuable services and *advice* we offer? Doesn't everyone want conflict-free advice?

We do so much for our clients, and our experience has taught us they value our advice and are willing to pay for more services. We know this. We encourage you to separate your IA services from your planning to avoid a conflict of interest. Let's charge the appropriate fees for the value of our ongoing professional advice.

Financial-Planning Client-Service Calendar

On the next page is an example of an annual financial-planning client-service calendar we use at North Star.

It lists topics you can discuss with your clients for each month of the year. It is a useful tool for adding client touchpoints to your calendar. This will tie into your client-service model you have implemented, based on your client segmentation.

Sample Annual Financial-Planning Client-Service Calendar

January	February	March	April	May	June
Update Client Profile in CRM including important goals	Update financial planning projections and goal tracking	Quarterly newsletter	Check in on ongoing financial planning tasks**	Educational event for clients/ prospects	Quarterly newsletter
Annual investment performance report and review	Capital gains tax reporting summary	Update college funding projections	Prior quarter investment performance report	Employee benefits review	Annual insurance protection review and update
Annual budgeting and debt review	Excess cash review	IRA contribution check-in		Review client tax returns for planning input	Mid-year progress review against goals
		Update retirement projections			

July	August	September	October	November	December
Prior quarter investment performance report	Check in on ongoing financial planning tasks	Quarterly newsletter	Educational event for clients/ prospects	Estate planning review*	Quarterly newsletter
Mid-year cash flow check-in	Suggest to check annual credit score	Property and casualty review	Prior quarter investment performance report	End of year tax considerations*	Employee benefit review
Review 401k and investment accounts	Semi-annual budgeting and debt review	Long-term care and Medicare review	Required Minimum Distribution review	Compensation review and benchmarking	401k election review

North Star Professional Center – 2701 University Ave SE, Minneapolis, MN 55414

*Financial Advisors do not provide tax or legal advice. Please consult a tax or legal professional for advice regarding your specific tax or legal situation.
This is an example of what a year may look like over the course of a financial planning relationship. Your level of services and timing for services may vary. Separate from the financial plan and our role as financial planner, we may recommend the purchase of specific investment or insurance products or accounts. These product recommendations are not part of the financial plan and you are under no obligation to follow them.

Securities and investment advisory services offered through Securian Financial Services, Inc. Member FINRA/SIPC. North Star Resource Group is independently owned and operated.
2739873 / DOFU 02/2020

Commissions Might Someday Disappear Altogether

This chapter on practice economics would not be complete without a discussion of a worldwide trend to ban commissions.

Several countries have placed outright bans on some commissions in an effort to align incentives between financial advisors and their clients, and several have raised professional standards required to become a financial advisor. The goal is to standardize the quality of service financial advisors provide to their clients and to ensure they act in their clients' best interests.

India was one of the first countries to institute bans. In 2009, India banned up-front commissions on open-ended mutual funds. In 2012, Australia instituted Future Of Financial Advice (FOFA) reforms, which ultimately led to a ban on investment commissions as well.[41]

And then, in 2013, the United Kingdom implemented its Retail Distribution Review (RDR), which led to a ban on investment commissions in the UK. The Dutch implemented a commission-ban that year as well.

Here at home, the US Department of Labor (DOL) fiduciary rule, which has not yet become law, has a similar intent.

The rule was originally scheduled to be phased in from April 10, 2017, to January 1, 2018. As of June 21, 2018, though, the US Fifth Circuit Court of Appeals officially vacated the rule, effectively killing it. However, former Department of Labor Secretary Alexander Acosta stated in May 2019 that the DOL was working with the SEC to resurrect the fiduciary rule.[42] As of June 2022, there was still no final guidance on enforcement.

The DOL's definition of *fiduciary* demands that retirement advisors act in the best interests of their clients and put their

41. "How the Fiduciary Movement Became a Global Phenomenon," Michael Kitces, August 24, 2017, Kitces.com, https://www.kitces.com/blog/fiduciary-movement-global-phenomenon-dol-rdr-fofa-crm2/.
42. "Everything You Need to Know About the DOL Fiduciary Rule," Katelyn Peters, Investopedia, updated July 14, 2021, https://www.investopedia.com/updates/dol-fiduciary-rule/.

clients' interests above their own. It leaves no room for advisors to conceal any potential conflict of interest and states that all fees and commissions for retirement plans and retirement-planning advice must be clearly disclosed in dollar form to clients.[43]

The definition was expanded to include any professional making a recommendation or solicitation in this area, not simply giving ongoing advice. Previously, only advisors who were charging a fee for service (either hourly or as a percentage of account holdings) were likely to be fiduciaries.[44]

The rule applies only to advisors' recommendations on retirement-related investments.

Now, we believe professional advisors who have a strong sense of purpose are perfectly capable of acting in their clients' best interests without having the government mandate them to do so. Yet because of the actions of a few "bad applies" who have taken advantage of clients over the years, the flurry of potential legislation continues worldwide.

Advisors are required by law to always put their clients' best interests first, and they cannot sell their clients investment products that do not align with their needs, objectives, and risk tolerance. They must conduct a thorough analysis of investments before making recommendations, disclose any conflict of interest, and use the best execution of trades when investing.[45]

Obviously, if commissions are banned, advisors will have to move to a fee-based compensation model.

The Shoemaker's Children Should Have Shoes

Maybe you've heard the old adage, "The cobbler's children have no shoes." According to this proverb, often, professionals get so busy serving their customers or clients that they neglect their

43. Ibid.
44. Ibid.
45. "Fee-Based vs. Commission-Based: What's the Difference?" Barclay Palmer, Investopedia, reviewed on June 30, 2021, https://www.investopedia.com/articles/basics/04/022704.asp.

needs of those of those closest to them. In this case, the story was about a cobbler, or shoemaker, whose children had no shoes because he was so busy making shoes for his customers.

This adage should not apply to advisors. Just as the shoemaker's children need to have shoes, financial advisors need to have their financial houses in order.

Our profession is unfortunately populated by too many advisors who do not manage their own money well; do not have sufficient, or sometimes any, life insurance in place; or do not create personal wealth. Advisors are business owners and need to have financial plans for themselves. They need to pay themselves a salary and save the remainder in retirement accounts.

I worked with a group of advisors who prepared financial plans for each other. This assured another set of eyes on their situations and provided greater accountability. Advisors should and can take their own advice to do the same good work for themselves they do for their best clients. When we follow our own guidelines, we elevate our profession.

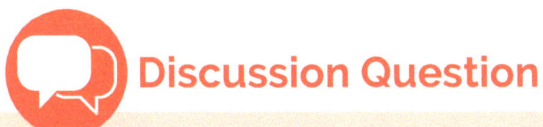 **Discussion Question**

Have you ever neglected your own financial well-being because you didn't make it a priority? Are there any steps you need to take right now to follow the advice you give your clients? Set a deadline for yourself to get your own financial house in order.

Business Continuation: Ensure Your Practice Continues Changing Lives, Forever

Most successful advisors spend years, often decades, building their businesses. Those practices are composed of hundreds of families and business owners who rely on the advisors, their teams, and their practice to be the guardians of their financial future.

None of us is immortal. At some point, the founding advisor cannot or will not be here any longer. We have met many advisors who just don't know how to quit. We have also taken over practices whose advisors are suddenly and unexpectedly gone because of a crippling disability or death. As advisors, we tend to excel at preparing our clients for these events in their own lives and careers, yet we do not always do this for ourselves.

This is where business continuation plans come into place. We prefer the term "businesses continuation" over "succession planning." The business can and will go on if there are even basic plans in place.

At North Star, we have two approaches to this dilemma. First, we have available an agreement between our advisors and the firm whereby the firm purchases the advisor's recurring revenue in the event of disability or death. Admittedly and purposely, the multiple is low; it is meant to be a foundational value, a placeholder until a market-priced agreement can be put in place.

Second, we also provide templates so two or more advisors can make an agreement to buy each other out as a living transition upon a death or disability. It provides greater value to the exiting advisor and allows for more input and control. This is a complex topic, and there are some great books on the subject—most notably Mark Tibergien and Owen Dahl's book titled *How to Value, Buy, or Sell a Financial Advisory Practice: A Manual on Mergers, Acquisitions, and Transition Planning*.

Before we move from this topic, we want to mention a very

successful program we have in place; we call it "advisor adoption," and you are welcome to copy it. In 2018 Ed Deutschlander teamed up with Patrick Leary of LIMRA to research and publish a white paper called "Adoption: Solving for the Retention, Practice Continuation, and Talent Shortage Challenge within the Financial Services Profession."

The notion here is that a veteran advisor identifies an early career advisor to take into his or her practice. We often have several dozen advisors in our early career program who are candidates. Some want to build their practices on their own and do it their way. Others want to team with a senior advisor. In those cases, the senior advisor takes on the responsibility to make sure the junior advisor meets all validation and training requirements. We recruit, select, license, and develop the advisors to get them to be attractive adoption candidates. We host social get-togethers for the veterans to meet these early career talents. It's like an internal job fair.

This is an incredibly successful program. It's not a mystery why advisors who are "adopted" have a much higher success rate than "do-it-yourself" advisors.

Adding junior advisors to a veteran practice not only increases their capacity and, in some cases, expertise like financial advice; it also provides candidates for business continuation scenarios. Teaming and building multiple advisor/team-member practices are the future. To us, they are firms within the firm that enable us to leverage each other's talents and resources.

Discussion Question

What is your business continuation plan? If you do not have one, or if it is not up-to-date and sufficient to optimize your practice's ability to continue serving your clients in your absence, make it a priority to develop one. Consider taking advantage of North Star's "advisor adoption" program.

CHAPTER 8

AN IDEA WHOSE TIME HAS COME

> "Nothing is as powerful as an idea whose time has come."

Victor Hugo

We advocate that ongoing comprehensive financial advice for a fee with top-segment clients is an idea whose time has come. Everything we see in the contemporary financial advisor–client relationship reinforces this urgency.

The following are two examples from history that illustrate ideas whose time had come. Both have continued to impact the world in significant ways.

1. Gutenberg Printing Press

German goldsmith Johannes Gutenberg is credited with inventing the printing press around 1436, although he was far from the first to automate the book-printing process. Woodblock printing in China dates back to the ninth century, and Korean bookmakers were printing with moveable metal type a century before Gutenberg.[46]

---

46. "7 Ways the Printing Press Changed the World," Dave Roos, History.com, updated September 3, 2019, https://www.history.com/news/printing-press-renaissance.

But still, everything before was done by hand. This was a game changer. A printing press could create many more copies at a faster rate than even the best scribes. Printing could reach more people, over a wider area, than one person to instruct or teach others. Knowledge passed on orally or from scribe to scribe had grown increasingly fragmentary and corrupted over time. The printing press made it possible to collect and organize knowledge and pass it on intact. It altered how people learned, shared knowledge, spread opinions, and amused themselves. It allowed the masses to have access to knowledge, the same as the elites. It was the internet of the Renaissance.

2. Whale Oil, Kerosene, and Gasoline

In the mid-1800s, whale oil was the lamp and lighting fuel choice for Americans. Rising costs and difficulty getting whale oil led to a search for alternatives. At the turn of the century, oil refineries' primary objective was to extract kerosene to fuel lamps. The use of electric lights superseded this practice decades later. In the meantime, kerosene production resulted in a highly flammable volatile by-product—gasoline. People disposed of this unwanted by-product without a thought. They poured it on the ground and into our waterways.

John D. Rockefeller of the Standard Oil Company realized the potential of gasoline and began to market it to the nascent auto industry, which was looking at steam, electricity, and kerosene to fuel early automobiles. Gasoline was cheap, easy to obtain, and produced relatively high power.[47]

The rest, we say, is history. The time had come. Ironically, it is now electric vehicles that are a significant competitor to internal combustion engines.

---

47. Different sources provide different variations on the history of whale oil, kerosene, and gasoline. One source is "Petroleum Technology History, Part 1—Background," at Great Achievements.org, http://www.greatachievements.org/?id=3677. Another is "Gasoline Explained: History of Gasoline," US Energy Information Administration (EIA), https://www.eia. gov/energyexplained/gasoline/history-of-gasoline.php.

While these two examples may seem unrelated, we suggest they are prescriptive. This book has presented the case of the value of a client and advisor working in a framework of financial advice and planning to advance the financial security and preparedness of alert and receptive clients. Once they see its value, they would not want to work another way. It is an idea whose time has come.

What We Know About Planning Clients

Advice clients appreciate our knowledge and wisdom. We know they are more engaged in the process of gaining financial traction. They take our advice. They refer more people to us. They may have a higher level of financial goal achievement. What a great outcome for advice clients—and for their advisors!

When you focus on advice, you deepen your professional relationships with your clients. You are their financial "lifeguard," watching out for them and leading them to make wise decisions about their money.

In 2018, Dr. Moira Somers published a book titled *Advice That Sticks: How to Give Financial Advice That People Will Follow*. Dr. Somers is a neuropsychologist, professor, and executive coach in the field of financial psychology and financial change.

In her book, she reveals why some clients take their advisors' financial advice, while others don't. Her research shows that when clients do not take our advice, "it's rarely because the advisor is technically unskilled or incorrect," she writes. "Instead, it's usually because the personal side of things has been neglected or misread."[48]

This is not surprising, Dr. Somers says, because financial advisors receive vast training on the technical side of the business

48. Dr. Moira Somers, *Advice That Sticks: How to Give Financial Advice That People Will Follow* (Bramley, Tadley, United Kingdom: Practical Inspiration Publishing, 2018).

but very little training on client psychology—the personal aspect of working with clients.

Once you see yourself as a valuable partner to your clients, paying attention to their worries, concerns, hopes and dreams, they will become more engaged with you, too.

The Impact of Planning

As an advisor, you are aware that the most pervasive financial worry among our clients is they will run out of money in retirement. The COVID-19 pandemic increased this worry for most Americans.

Your financial advice eases people's worry about running out of money. That is a significant impact only you can make, as their financial advisor.

More than three in four Americans (77 percent) reported feeling anxious about their financial situation. Their concerns ranged from savings and retirement to affording a house or a child's education. This information is from the "Mind over Money" survey that Capital One and The Decision Lab released at in 2020.

More specifically, the study showed that Americans are most worried about their financial future, which includes not having enough money to retire (68 percent), keeping up with the cost of living (56 percent), and managing debt levels (45 percent). These financial worries affect people's health negatively. The report noted that 43 percent of the survey respondents felt fatigued, 42 percent found it difficult to concentrate at work, 41 percent had trouble sleeping, and 25 percent said financial stress was affecting their relationships.[49]

If you desire to change lives, imagine the impact you can have by providing financial advice and the peace of mind that comes with that.

---

49. "77% of Americans Are Anxious About Their Financial Situation—Here's How to Take Control," Alexandria White, CNBC, updated October 30, 2020, https://www.cnbc.com/select/how-to-take-control-of-your-finances/.

Prudential has done a great job of advocating financial advice with its advisors. I recently saw a billboard near our office in Minneapolis that said this:

> Worrying about retirement takes
> more energy than planning for it.

Isn't that true? Regardless of what life stage people are in, the overriding worry that most of them have is *not having enough money*. This is a common concern, even among high-net-worth clients. Many people feel embarrassed about revealing this worry to professional advisors; they believe they "should" be more successful than they are. They fear being judged.

I saw another statement recently that is equally compelling:

> How do you plan for retirement?
> What if it comes early?

That's a second worry many people have. Not only do they wonder if they will run out of money once they decide to retire; they also worry if they have to retire before they're ready. The COVID-19 pandemic amplified this worry, with retirement coming early for many people whose companies shut down, suffered layoffs, or faced other unexpected circumstances.

You Will Facilitate Your Clients' Ability to Have an Impact

Now, although most people worry about running out of money, most people are not afraid of dying. They are afraid of passing away without their lives having sufficient meaning. When you build relationships with your clients and learn what matters to them, you can facilitate the intersection between their values and their assets. This is a priceless service. No robo-advisor can provide that. No app can do that. You alone can give that gift to your clients.

A woman named Bronnie Ware worked in palliative care with patients who were dying. She noticed five common regrets that her patients voiced as their lives were coming to a close. She listed those top five regrets in her 2019 book *The Top Five Regrets of the Dying: A Life Transformed by the Dearly Departing*, which has been translated into twenty-nine languages. Here are the top five regrets people expressed at the end of their lives:[50]

1. "I wish I'd had the courage to live a life true to myself, not the life others expected of me."
2. "I wish I hadn't worked so hard."
3. "I wish I'd had the courage to express my feelings."
4. "I wish I had stayed in touch with my friends."
5. "I wish I had let myself be happier."

As your clients' financial advisor, you are uniquely equipped to coach them to make the choices that will enable them to avoid those regrets. That alone makes your advice and support priceless.

Discussion Question

What regrets do you have at this point in your life, if any? What regrets have your clients expressed? How can being aware of these regrets lead your clients, and you, to take actions and adopt behaviors needed to address the regrets?

---

50. Bronnie Ware, *The Top Five Regrets of the Dying: A Life Transformed by the Dearly Departing* (Carlsbad, California: Hay House, Inc.) August 13, 2019.

Your Practice on Purpose

In closing, we want to reiterate the uniquely valuable concept of what a Practice on Purpose is. Again, the term suggests a double meaning of the word "purpose"—you build your practice around your personal *purpose*, and you build it in an intentional way, on *purpose*.

It also means adapting to change to ensure your practice continues to serve your clients optimally, regardless of what happens in the world, the economy, or in your own life. I recently finished reading a book about the history of China. In it is a story about an emperor who was advising his son. The son asked his father, "What is the most important lesson for me?"

The emperor replied, "Make friends with change."

I think that is a beautiful phrase, and it is wise advice for us all.

Throughout this second edition of *Practice on Purpose*, we have urged you to think about, and determine, what your Practice on Purpose will look like. If you haven't yet completed your purpose statement, we encourage you to do so. It will serve as the foundation for every decision you make and every action you take as you build the practice you desire and your clients deserve.

The following is another example of a purpose statement you can borrow from and modify as needed. It contains the key elements of a Practice on Purpose:

Sample Purpose Statement
for a Practice on Purpose

As an advisor, I will make a significant and positive difference in the lives of our clients and their families by ensuring that, in my Practice on Purpose:

- We prepare for the certainty of uncertainty.

- Our clients are protected along the way in the event of disability, illness, or untimely death.

- We ensure our clients always have a safe and ready source of money if they need it for emergencies or opportunities.

- We contribute to our clients' families having lives full of the things that matter to them—homes, travel, education, charitable giving, confident retirements, and estate creation.

- Our clients are better off because they worked with our practice.

- Our practice always aligns with my values, and we run it *on* purpose and *with* a purpose.

- The practice becomes a significant asset for me in my retirement, and I will leave a legacy and capable successors to continue providing quality advice to our clients and their children.

The Cycle of an Advisor's Practice on Purpose

The following diagram illustrates the possible life cycle of a Practice on Purpose. It includes many key concepts from this book and was included in the workbook from the first edition. It's a great visual of how the components of a Practice on Purpose build on each other and the connectivity between them. This is not a static journey. How often have we seen practices reinvent themselves as they grow or as the advisor grows as a person? We are in the endless pursuit of getting better.

We hope this visual is inspirational and instructive. Through doing good for others, we will have done well for ourselves. When we know and live our purpose, our best years are always ahead of us. Take care.

Practice Life Cycle

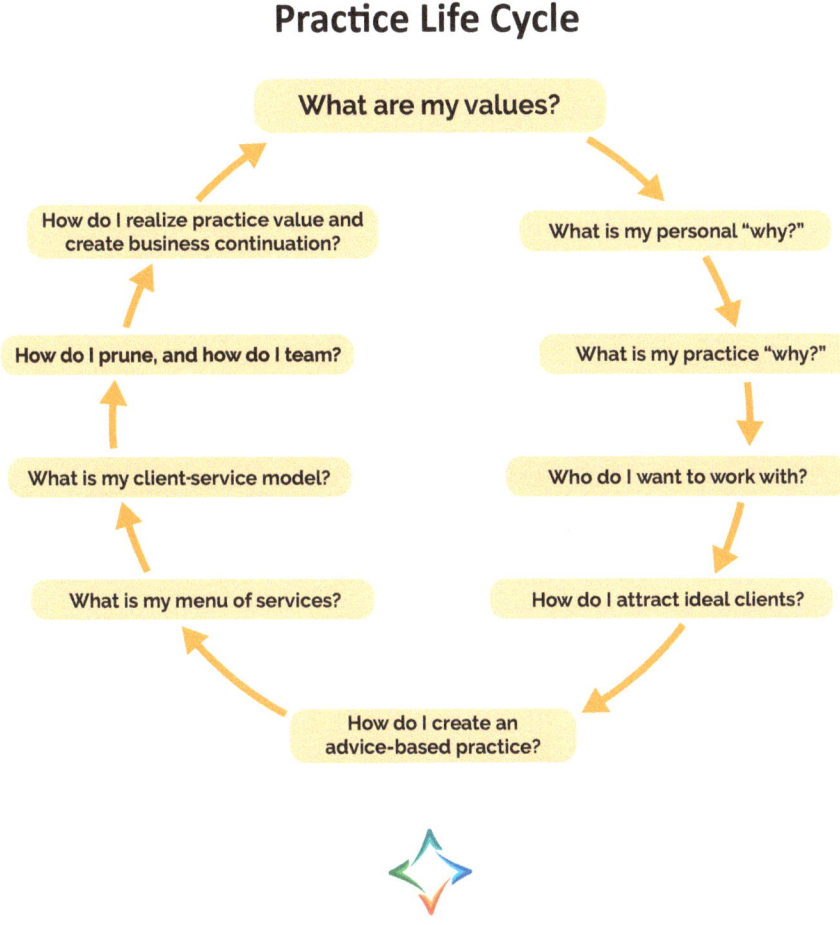

On behalf of all of us at North Star Resource Group, we sincerely thank you for all you do for our profession; for each other; and most of all, for the families and businesses whose lives we have changed for the better—forever.

APPENDIX

Suggested Reading

Author(s)	Book Title
Mitch Anthony and Paul Armson	*Life Centered Financial Planning: How to Deliver Value That Will Never Be Under-valued*
Bill Bachrach	*Values-Based Financial Planning: The Art of Creating an Inspiring Financial Strategy*
Ben G. Baldwin	*The New Life Insurance Investment Advisor: Achieving Financial Security for You and Your Family Through Today's Insurance Products*
Paul Batz and Tim Schmidt,	*What Really Works: Blending the Seven F's for the Life You Imagine*
Jeb Blount	*Virtual Selling: A Quick-Start Guide to Leveraging Video, Technology, and Virtual Communication Channels to Engage Remote Buyers and Close Deals Fast*
Russell H. Conwell and John Wanamaker	*Acres of Diamonds: Life-Changing Classics*
Chris Crowley and Henry S. Lodge, MD	*Younger Next Year: Live Strong, Fit, and Sexy—Until You're 80 and Beyond*
Donna Skeels Cygan	*The Joy of Financial Security: The Art and Science of Becoming Happier, Managing Your Money Wisely, and Creating a Secure Financial Future*
Edward G. Deutschlander and Rich Campe	*Be the First Believer: Leadership Life Lessons*

Author(s)	Book Title
Roy DiLiberto	*Basic Truths for Financial Life Planners*
Roy DiLiberto	*Financial Planning: The Next Step: A Practical Approach to Merging Your Clients' Money with Their Lives*
Ken Dychtwald and Robert Morison	*What Retirees Want: A Holistic View of Life's Third Age*
Tom Hegna	*Paychecks and Playchecks: Retirement Solutions for Life*
Morgan Housel and Chris Hill	*The Psychology of Money: Timeless Lessons on Wealth, Greed, and Happiness*
Joe Jordan	*Living a Life of Significance*
Troy Korsgaden	*Power Position Your Agency: A Guide to Insurance Agency Success*
Troy Korsgaden	*Profit from Change: Retooling Your Agency for Maximum Profits*
Richard J. Leider	*The Power of Purpose: Creating Meaning in Your Life and Work*
Douglas Lennick, Roy Geer, and Ryan Goulart	*Leveraging Your Financial Intelligence: At the Intersection of Money, Health, and Happiness*
Doug Lennick with Kathleen Jordan, PhD	*Financial Intelligence: How to Make Smart, Values-Based Decisions with Your Money and Your Life*
Duncan MacPherson and Chris Jeppesen	*The Advisor Playbook: Regain Liberation and Order in Your Personal and Professional Life*
Nick Murray	*Behavioral Investment Counseling*
Nick Murray	*The Game of Numbers: Client Acquisition for Financial Advisors*
Nick Murray	*The New Financial Advisor*
Nick Murray and John Murray	*Talking It Over, Just the Two of Us: A Guide for the Financial Advisor's Life Partner*

Author(s)	Book Title
Phillip Palaveev	*The Ensemble Practice: A Team-Based Approach*
Alan Parisse and David Richman	*Questions Great Financial Advisors Ask… And Investors Need to Know*
Carl Richards	*The Behavior Gap, Simple Ways to Stop Doing Dumb Things with Money*
Phillip C. Richards	*Twenty-Five Secrets to Sustainable Success*
Phillip C. Richards and Dr. Jarrod Spencer	*The Sky Is Not the Limit: Discovering the True North for Your Life's Path*
Vicki Robin and Joe Dominguez	*Your Money or Your Life: 9 Steps to Transforming Your Relationship with Money and Achieving Financial Independence*
Dr. Moira Somers	*Advice That Sticks: How to Give Financial Advice That People Will Follow*
Dan Sullivan	*The Good That Financial Advisors Do*
Mark C. Tibergien and Owen Dahl	*How to Value, Buy, or Sell a Financial Advisory Practice: A Manual on Mergers, Acquisitions, and Transition Planning*
Mark C. Tibergien and Kim G. Dellarocca	*The Enduring Advisory Firm: How to Serve Your Clients More Effectively and Operate More Efficiently*
Mark C. Tibergien and Rebecca Pomering	*Practice Made More Perfect: Transforming a Financial Advisory Practice into a Business*

ABOUT THE AUTHORS

Gary H. Schwartz, CLU®, ChFC®, CRPC®
Executive Vice President
North Star Resource Group

gary@northstarfinancial.com
(612) 617-6029

As North Star Resource Group's Executive Vice President, Gary Schwartz provides professional consulting services to senior financial professionals on developing their teams, succession planning, and leading million-dollar practices.

Gary joined North Star in 2013, bringing with him more than thirty years of experience managing financial representatives' growth at Minnesota Mutual, Securian Financial Services, and Ameriprise Financial Services. He worked for four years as Senior Vice President of Advisor Growth and Development before being promoted to EVP in 2017.

He specializes in developing practice-management analytics to improve the productivity and effectiveness of a financial practice. Gary's strategies are outlined in his book, *Practice on Purpose: Achieve the Financial Advice Practice You Desire and Your Clients Deserve* (first edition, 2014; second edition, 2022).

Beyond his work in individual firms, Gary is also an active contributor to the financial services profession on topics of coaching financial professionals and building practices. Within professional organizations, Gary is past chair of LIMRA's Career Agency Building Committee and Securian's ambassador and diplomat to GAMA International. He worked as an adjunct professor emeritus for the University of St. Thomas Graduate School of Business and is a regular presenter for GAMA International, speaking to financial professionals throughout the world.

A long-time Minnesota local, Gary earned his bachelor's degree from the University of Minnesota, where he was active as a Martin Luther King Economics tutor and was elected to the student governing board of the business school. He later earned a master's degree in industrial psychology from the University of Minnesota.

Gary and his family live in Prior Lake, Minnesota., where he enjoys time on the lake, outdoor sports, and reading books on leadership and business. Gary also takes time to travel, especially to visit family in Seattle.

He is a Registered Representative and Investment Advisor Representative of Securian Financial Services, Inc.

Phillip C. Richards, CLU®, RHU®
Executive Chairman and Founder
North Star Resource Group

phil.richards@northstarfinancial.com
(612) 617-6167

Phillip C. Richards is the Executive Chairman and founder of the affiliated companies that comprise North Star Resource Group. North Star represents a fully integrated array of financial services and products for individuals and businesses of all sizes and has more than 150,000 product placements with clients with offices in 22 states with client assets under administration exceeding $10 billion.[51]

Phil earned his bachelor of science in 1962 from Temple University, where he served as student body president and received the prestigious Sword Award as outstanding senior classman. A recipient of a four-year wrestling scholarship, he served as team captain and was inducted into the National Wrestling Hall of Fame in 2010 and the National High School Coaches Hall of Fame in 2010. Phil was elected to the Temple University Board of Trustees in 2009. In 2016, he was the commencement speaker for Temple University and was awarded an honorary Doctor of Humane Letters Degree. In 2019, Temple University appointed Phil as the vice chair to the board of trustees and the chair of the executive committee.

He began his professional career in 1962 with the Penn Mutual Life Insurance Company in Philadelphia. In 1965, he joined Hartford Life, leading the company in sales. In 1969, Phil acquired North Star Resource Group, which has received the prestigious Master Firm

---

51. As of December 31, 2020.

Award from GAMA International (now known as Finseca) every year since 1973. North Star is celebrating more than 114 years in business, with origins tracing back to 1908. The organization has been awarded the Charitable Champions award from Invest in Others in 2019[52]; the Community Leader award from *InvestmentNews* in 2010; and the Better Business Bureau of Minnesota and North Dakota's Torch Award for Ethics in 2011, 2015, and 2019[53], making the firm the only three-time winner in the region.

A winner of numerous awards in the profession, Phil is the 2005 inductee into the FINSECA (formerly GAMA International) Hall of Fame and is the only firm leader in the world to have received the International Management Award from FINSECA (formerly GAMA International) every year (forty-six years)[54] since the inception of that award. In 2007, Phil was named the recipient of the 66th annual John Newton Russell Memorial Award[55], the highest honor in the insurance profession by the National Association of Insurance and Financial

52. North Star Resource Group received the Master Firm Award from GAMA International (now known as Finseca) from 1987 to2021. The ranking is based on achieving a predetermined level of premiums and commissions, as well as maintaining good compliance standing with Finseca. This ranking includes only firms that paid an application fee. Working with this firm is not a guarantee of future financial results. Investors should conduct their own evaluations.

53. North Star Resource Group was a firm that was awarded the Torch Award for Marketplace Ethics by the Better Business Bureau of MN & ND in 2019. Companies were evaluated in categories based on number of employees. In order to be eligible for the award, firms must be in business for three years or longer, earn an "A" rating from the BBB, meet financial obligations and not have won the award in the past three years. Working with this firm is not a guarantee of future financial results. Investors should conduct their own evaluation.

54. Up-to-date as of 2021. Finseca is a membership organization for which individuals must submit applications and payment. The organization is geared toward those in recruiting, training, or supervision roles in the financial services industry. Awards are based primarily on commissions, premiums, or fees generated from investment and insurance products and other criteria relative to leadership, achievement, and recruiting selected by the applicant. Individuals must be current with membership dues and submit an application fee for consideration. Working with this individual is not a guarantee of future financial results. Investors should conduct their own evaluations.

55. Phillip Richards received the John Newton Russell Memorial Award in 2007. Individuals were nominated by peers and evaluated based on criteria such as character, dedication to the profession, meritorious service, a detailed biography, and peer letters of recommendation. Working with this firm is not a guarantee of future financial results. Investors should conduct their own evaluations.

Advisors (NAIFA). He was inducted into The American College of Financial Services Hall of Fame in 2016 and the Insurance Business America Hall of Fame in 2020.

Phil's first book, *25 Secrets for Sustainable Success*, was published in 2007 with the expectation that it will continue to be adopted by many as the gold standard for the profession. He has since cowritten *The Sky Is Not the Limit* (2014), *Practice on Purpose* (2015 and 2022), and *Promises Kept* (2016).

Phil is an adjunct professor emeritus for the Carlson School of Management at the University of Minnesota and a former adjunct professor at Central University of Finance and Economics in Beijing. In addition, he is a four-time chairman of Securian's National Advisory Board and was inducted into Securian's Hall of Fame as the nineteenth member.[56] He served on the Executive Board of Directors for the Minnesota Council for Quality and is a past president of FINSECA (formerly GAMA International) (2003).

He is a forty-five-year arbitrator for the Better Business Bureau, is a past chairman of the Better Business Bureau of Minnesota and North Dakota Board of Directors, served on the Arizona Quality Council Board of Directors, and served on The American College Board of Trustees in Philadelphia for nine years. In 2016, he was inducted into The College's Hall of Fame in New York City.

In addition, he is a past chairman of the LIFE Foundation and currently serves on the Mayo Clinic of Arizona Leadership Council and on the Board of the National High School Coaches Association, and he is a past treasurer of the Arizona Heart Foundation Board of Trustees. He chairs the Scott Richards North Star Foundation, which annually receives 10 percent of all North Star's profits, and has

---

56. Phillip Richards was inducted into the Securian Hall of Fame in 2012. Candidates eligible for consideration must have not been under contract or employed by Securian Financial Services, Inc., for a period of two years or attain the age of 67. Candidates are evaluated based on commissions, premiums, or fees generated from investment and insurance products and other criteria relative to leadership, achievement, and recruiting. Working with this firm is not a guarantee of future financial results. Investors should conduct their own evaluations.

given more than $5.8 million to charities since 2004.[57] Since 2018, the foundation has funded two seven-figure endowed chairs for Alzheimer's research at the Lewis Katz Temple Medical Center.

Phil has been a featured speaker in seventeen countries, on topics including strategic planning, leadership, and alternate distribution systems in the financial services profession in the twenty-first century. He has addressed the annual meetings of more than 150 major companies; was a main-platform speaker at the National GAMA International LAMP Meeting in 1998 and its Canadian counterpart in Toronto in 1999; was a main-platform speaker in Singapore, Taipei, and Manila in August 2000; and was a main-platform speaker at the Asian Pacific Conference in Bangkok (where he cofounded GAMA Thailand) in 2001 and 2010; Singapore in 2011 and 2015; Crete, Greece, in 2002; Athens, Greece, in 2006, 2010, and 2015; Sydney, Australia, in 2005; and Buenos Aires, Argentina. He has spoken in Shanghai and Beijing numerous times as a lecturer at Beijing University and Shanghai University for Finance and Economics.

He was a main-platform speaker for MDRT in Vancouver in 2010 and in Ireland in 2012, as well as GAMA LAMP Asia in 2014 and 2016. He was a 2016 Asia LAMP main-platform speaker in Bangkok and was a featured speaker in Vietnam and Singapore in 2016 and again in Bangkok and Singapore in 2017 and 2019.

Phil is a registered representative and investment advisor representative of Securian Financial Services, Inc.

_____

57. As of June 26, 2020.

Ed Deutschlander, CLU®, CLF®
Chief Executive Officer
North Star Resource Group

ed@northstarfinancial.com

Ed Deutschlander has been the CEO at North Star Resource Group since 2016.

He began his career at North Star just days after college graduation. He worked for one year as a financial advisor, but he quickly found his gifts were better used in the recruiting department, where he was soon promoted to National Recruiting Director and then transitioned into greater leadership roles within the firm. Having experienced the profession as an advisor, recruiter, and now executive, Ed brings a unique, multifaceted perspective to his leadership.

With Ed's clear focus on values and ethical practices, North Star has received several prestigious awards, including Top Workplaces USA (2021), the *Star Tribune*'s Top Workplaces (2016), *Minnesota Business Magazine*'s Best Companies to Work For (2015), Charitable Champions by *InvestmentNews* (2015, 2016, and 2019), and the Better Business Bureau's Torch Awards for Ethics (2011, 2015, and

2019)[58], among many others.

Individually, Ed has been recognized for his excellence in leadership in the profession and community, including *Minnesota Business Magazine*'s Community Impact Award and the Paragon of Leadership award.

Ed is a contributor in the financial services profession as the secretary of the Finseca board of directors, immediate past chair of the Finseca Foundation's executive committee, and member of the board of trustees for The American College.

In terms of community service, Ed serves as a founding member of the Scott Richards North Star Foundation, which donates 10 percent of North Star's annual profits to national and local nonprofits. He is a founding board member for Bikes for Kids, a Minnesota-based nonprofit that has gifted more than five thousand bicycles and helmets since 2004.

A Midwest native and a 1993 graduate of Macalester College in St. Paul, Minnesota, Ed played, started, and lettered in varsity football and baseball and served as captain of the football team. He now works and lives in Austin, Texas, with his wife of twenty-eight years, Toni, along with their four children and four rescue dogs.

He is a registered representative and investment advisor representative of Securian Financial Services, Inc.

---

58. North Star Resource Group is a firm that was awarded the Torch Award for Marketplace Ethics by the Better Business Bureau of MN & ND in 2011, 2015, and 2020. Companies were evaluated in categories based on number of employees. To be eligible for the award, firms must be in business for three years or longer, earn an "A" rating from the BBB, meet financial obligations, and not have won the award in the past three years. Working with this firm is not a guarantee of future financial results. Investors should conduct their own evaluations. Financial Professionals do not provide tax or legal advice and this should not be considered as such. Please consult a tax or legal professional for advice regarding your specific situation. North Star Resource Group, 2701 University Ave SE, Minneapolis, MN 55414. Securities and investment advisory services offered through Securian Financial Services, Inc. Member FINRA/SIPC. North Star Resource Group is independently owned and operated.4305850/DOFU 5-2022